Pennsylvania Scotch-Irish Society

Annual Meeting and Banquet of the Pennsylvania Scotch-Irish Society at...

Pennsylvania Scotch-Irish Society

Annual Meeting and Banquet of the Pennsylvania Scotch-Irish Society at...

ISBN/EAN: 9783744786270

Printed in Europe, USA, Canada, Australia, Japan

Cover: Foto ©ninafisch / pixelio.de

More available books at **www.hansebooks.com**

NINTH ANNUAL MEETING

AND

BANQUET

OF THE

PENNSYLVANIA
SCOTCH-IRISH SOCIETY

AT THE

HOTEL BELLEVUE, PHILADELPHIA

FEBRUARY 10th, 1898

PHILADELPHIA
ALLEN, LANE & SCOTT'S PRINTING HOUSE
1211-13 Clover Street
1899

OFFICERS.

PRESIDENT,
Justice Henry W. Williams.

FIRST VICE-PRESIDENT,
Mr. James Pollock.

SECOND VICE-PRESIDENT,
Hon. John Stewart.

SECRETARY AND TREASURER,
Mr. Charles L. McKeehan.

DIRECTORS AND MEMBERS OF COUNCIL:

Mr. A. K. McClure,
Mr. T. Elliott Patterson,
Rev. J. S. MacIntosh, D. D.,
Hon. R. M. Henderson,
Mr. J. Bayard Henry,
Mr. Samuel F. Houston,
Rev. Henry C. McCook, D. D.,
Hon. James A. Logan,

Hon. James Gay Gordon,
Hon. W. W. Porter,
Rev. S. D. McConnell, D. D.,
Mr. Robert Pitcairn,
Mr. William J. Latta,
Mr. C. Stuart Patterson,
Col. John Cassels,
Mr. William Righter Fisher.

COMMITTEES.

ON ADMISSION OF MEMBERS:

James Pollock, *Chairman*,
W. W. Porter,
C. S. Patterson,

Robert Pitcairn,
J. Bayard Henry,
Charles L. McKeehan.

FINANCE:
The Officers of the Society.

ON ENTERTAINMENTS:

John Stewart, *Chairman*,
A. K. McClure,

T. Elliott Patterson,
William J. Latta,

John Cassels.

HISTORY AND ARCHIVES:

Henry C. McCook, *Chairman*,
Samuel F. Houston,

J. S. MacIntosh,
R. M. Henderson.

PEN Diagram

	Hugh McCaffrey, President of Hibernian Society.	Hon. Joseph C. Ferguson.	Rev. Stephen W. Dana, D.D., President of New England Society.	Hon. R. M. Henderson.	Justice Henry W. Williams.	Frank Thomson.	Col. A. K. McClure.	Hon. Marcus A. Hanna.	Wm. Righter Fisher.	Dr. Ethelbert D. Warfield	
Wm. H. Scott.	x										**A**
Rev. Robt. Hunter, D.D.	x							x		A. E. Hubbard	
			x	Alexander Harding.						J. Ba	
				Dr. Alexander Wilson.	x						
Preston Parr.	x		x	T. Hoge Patterson.				x		W. W. Pusey.	
				R. A. Wright.	x						
John C. McKinney.	x		x	George Hay.				x		W. J. McClary	
				Dr. M. J. Wilson.	x					Dr.	
			x	J. P. Donaldson.				x		Frank Pyle.	
Andrew C. McGowin.	x			Robert Carson.	x					Thom	
			x	James Hay.				x		Wm Henders	
				Wilfred L. Stauffer.	x						
Rev. S.A. Gayley, D.D.	x		x	Edwin M. Smucker.				x		Wilson H. Br	
				Francis Magee.	x					Jo	
Dr. W. S. Stewart.	x			Charles Scott.				x		R. H. Patton.	
		E		Wm. Ivins, Jr.	x	**D**				Frai	
Dr. J. H.W. Chestnut.	x		x	Rev. A. N. Haggarty.				x		Jas. D. Brook	
			x	Chas. W. Henry.						James C	
Craig D. Ritchie.	x			Theo. C. Patterson.	x			x		George McKe	
			x	James A. Develin.						A. C	
Dr. S. McC. Hamill.	x			W. P. Smith, Jr.	x			x		Benjamin Alle Vice-Pres. St.	
			x	Dr. C. McClelland.						W	
				Fred. E. Wayman.	x						
Edgar Dudley Faries.	x		x	Dr. Randolph Faries.				x		J. A. McDowe	
				Wm. Browne.	x						
Thomas E. Baird.	x		x	F. L. Baily.				x		Robert Dornai	
			x	Rev. Jacob Le Roy, D. D.						Alle	
George B. Bonnell.	x			George Campbell.	x			x		William Ivins	
			x	John B. Morgan.						W	
A. S. Bolles.	x			Henry A. Fry.	x						
		Samuel F. Houston.				James Pollock.					

...YLVANIA SCOTC...

...the Banquet Table...

C. Stuart Patterson.	Hon. M. Y. Herrick.	Hon. John B. McPherson.	Hon. Wm. W. Porter.	Justice J. Brewster McCollum.	Hon. Wm. R. Hanna...
X	X	X	X	X	X

		X	J. E. Barr.	
...enry.	X		T. Elliott...	
		X	William Thomps...	
...loyd.	X		Joh...	
		X	P. P. Bowles.	
...Latta.	X		Dr. John F...	
		X	Wm. Hammersle...	
...Latta.	X		George G...	
		X	Rev. W. H. McCa...	
...Davis.	X		Robert...	
		X	Robt. S. Hamme...	
...Latta.	X		Hon. J. D...	
		X	John B. Stauffer	
...kerly.	X	C	W. M. M...	
		X	E. T. Postlethwa...	
...erton.	X		Dr. W...	
		X	Hon. Geo. F. Hu...	
...sson.	X		Chas....	
		X	W. A. Patton.	
s Soc.				
...Latta.	X		James M...	
		X	Hon. Wm. McA...	
...Rea.	X		Talbot Merc...	
		X	Col. John Cassel	
...orke.	X		John H...	
		X	George V. Masse...	
...rnes.	X		W. F...	
		X		

Capt. John P. Green.

PENNSYLVANIA SCOTCH-IRISH SOCIETY.
Diagram of the Banquet Tables, February 10th, 1898.

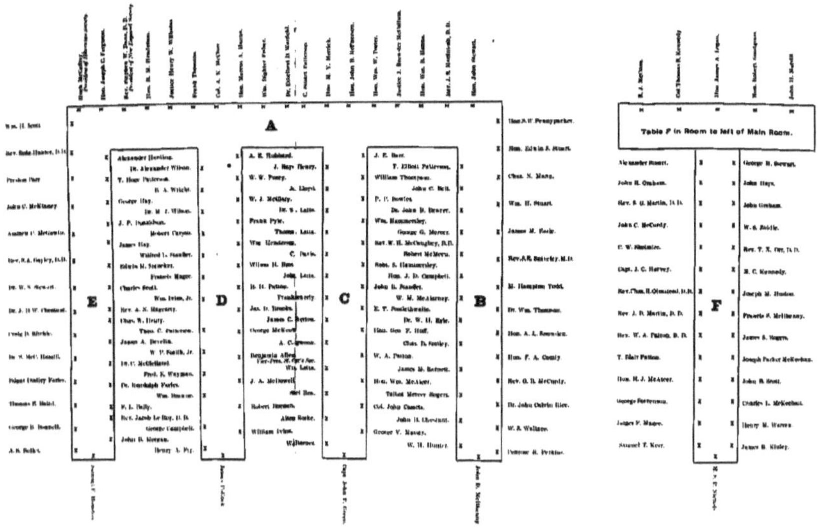

[Banquet seating chart showing six tables labeled A, B, C, D, E, and F, with Table F noted as being "in Room to left of Main Room." The head table A is at the top with dignitaries seated along it; tables B, C, D, E extend perpendicular from it in the main room.]

Head Table A (left to right):
Hugh McGaffrey; Hon. Joseph C. Ferguson; Rev. [illegible]; Hon. [illegible]; Rev. R. H. Henderson; James Henry M. Wilson; Hugh Thomson; Col. A. K. McClure; Hon. Martin G. Brumm; Hon. Stephen Collins; Hon. R. Chalfant D. Barfield; C. Stuart Patterson; Hon. H. V. Kerrick; Hon. John D. McPherson; Hon. James A. Beaver (Ex-Governor); Hon. Geo. B. Orlady; Hon. J. K. Rutherford, D.D.; Hon. John Stewart

Table F (separate room) — top header:
R. J. McGraw; Col. Thomas E. Kennedy; Hon. James A. Logan; Robert Snodgrass; John H. Bartell

---

Table E:
Wm. H. Scott
Rev. Robt Hunter, D.D.
Preston Platt
John C. McKinney
Andrew C. McGowan
Rev. R. A. Copley, D.D.
Dr. W. S. Stewart
Dr. J. H. W. Chestnut
Craig D. Ritchie
Dr. W. McC. Bissell
Peirpont Conley Porter
Thomas S. Heist
George D. Donnell
A. S. Bolles

Table D:
Alexander Hamilton
Dr. Alexander Wilson
T. Hess Patterson
D. A. Welsh
George Hay
Dr. M. J. Wilson
J. P. Donaldson
Robert Cowan
James Hay
Wilfred L. Saunders
Edwin M. Saunders
Francis Rager
Charles Scull
Wm. Irvine, Jr.
Rev. A. S. Shreeve
Chas. R. Drury
Thos. C. Patterson
James A. Develin
W. P. Smith, Jr.
Dr. C. McClelland
Fred. E. Waymen
Dr. Randolph Faries
Wm. Duncan
W. L. Duffy
Rev. Jacob Le Roy, D. D.
Geo. W. Campbell
John B. Keenan
Henry A. Fry

Table C:
A. R. Halstead
J. Bayr Henry
W. W. Posey
A. Lloyd
W. J. McGhey
Dr. N. S. Laios
Frank Pyle
Thomas Laios
Wm. Henderson
C. Paris
Wilson H. Rue
John Laios
D. H. Potson
Franklin Carty
Jas. D. Brooks
James C. Patton
George McKeon
A. C. Lamson
Benjamin Allen
Vice-Pres. McCoy's Anc.
Wm. Laios
J. A. McDowell
ditto Rue
Robert Howarth
Allen Burke
William Irwin
W. Thomas

Table B:
J. F. Barr
T. Elliott Patterson
William Thompson
John C. Bell
P. P. Bowles
Dr. John B. Deaver
Wm. Hammersley
George G. Mercer
Rev. W. H. McCaughey, D.D.
Robert McMurn
Robt. S. Hammersley
Hon. J. D. Campbell
John B. Sander
W. M. Mealarney
E. V. Penderthrales
Dr. W. H. Egle
Hon. Geo. F. Huff
Chas. D. Penley
W. A. Patton
Hon. F. A. Comly
Hon. Wm. McAleer
Tobias Mower Rogers
Col. John Caufle
John D. Chevaset
George V. Massey
W. H. Hunter

Table F (detail):
Alexander Reaser
John R. Graham
Rev. S. G. Martin, D. D.
John C. McCurdy
C. W. Mistatter
Capt. J. C. Harvey
Rev. Chas. R. Olmstead, D.D.
Rev. J. D. Martin, D. D.
Rev. W. A. Patton, D. D.
T. Blair Patton
Hon. H. J. McAteer
George Patterson
James F. Magee
Samuel T. Kerr
— — —
George B. Bergan
John Hays
John Graham
W. G. Biddle
Rev. T. X. Orr, D. D.
R. C. Kennedy
Joseph M. Huston
Pinerio S. McHenry
James S. Rogers
Joseph Parker McKeehan
John B. Scott
Charles L. McKeehan
Henry M. Warren
James R. Kinley

Table B head: Hon. Edwin S. Stuart
Table A end: Hon. S. W. Pennypacker
Right-side notes: Chas. N. Mann; Wm. H. Staart; James M. Beely; Rev. A.R. Batterby, M.D.; M. Hampton Todd; Dr. Wm. Thomson; Hon. A. L. Snowden; Rev. O. B. McCurdy; Dr. John Odvin Rice; W. S. Wallace; Former R. Pritbie

Note: Table F in Room to left of Main Room.

Ninth Annual Meeting.

The ninth annual meeting and banquet of the Pennsylvania Scotch-Irish Society was held at the Hotel Bellevue, Philadelphia, February 10th, 1898, Mr. William Righter Fisher in the chair.

The report of the Treasurer, Charles L. McKeehan, was presented and approved. (See Appendix D.)

Upon the nomination of Edwin S. Stuart, the following officers and Board of Directors were elected to serve for the ensuing year:—

President, JUSTICE HENRY W. WILLIAMS.
First Vice-President, MR. JAMES POLLOCK.
Second Vice-President, HON. JOHN STEWART.
Secretary and Treasurer, MR. CHARLES L. MCKEEHAN.
Directors and Members of Council:

HON. A. K. MCCLURE,	HON. W. W. PORTER,
MR. T. ELLIOTT PATTERSON,	HON. JAMES GAY GORDON,
REV. J. S. MACINTOSH, D.D.,	REV. S. D. MCCONNELL, D.D.
HON. R. M. HENDERSON,	MR. ROBERT PITCAIRN,
HON. J. BAYARD HENRY,	HON. C. STUART PATTERSON,
MR. SAMUEL F. HOUSTON,	COL. JOHN CASSELS,
REV. HENRY C. MCCOOK, D.D.,	MR. WILLIAM RIGHTER FISHER,
HON. JAMES A. LOGAN,	MR. WILLIAM J. LATTA.

On motion, the business meeting was then adjourned, and the company proceeded to the banquet room, where the President, Mr. William Righter Fisher, took the chair.

Rev. S. A. Gayley, D. D., invoked the Divine blessing.

At the close of the dinner Mr. William Righter Fisher, the President, arose and spoke as follows:—

GENTLEMEN AND BRETHREN OF THE SCOTCH-IRISH SOCIETY:—It is no part of my province this evening to make an extended speech. There is, however, one custom, which has lately obtained amongst us something of the force of law, which I wish to hand down, unimpaired, to my successors. It is, that each succeeding President should endeavor to pay the debt, which he owes to the honor of presiding here, by making some contribution of thought bearing upon the characteristic services of the Scotch-Irish race in molding the institutions of the country, or in giving temper and tone to its social life. I will detain you but a moment with what I have to say.

That distinguished scholar, historian, and biographer, Dr. C. J. Stillé, who lays no claim to Scotch-Irish extraction, after commenting, in his admirable life of John Dickinson, upon the deficiencies in the educational institutions of our early Colonial days, and particularly referring to the colleges of Harvard, of Yale, and of William and Mary, indulges in the following significant and pregnant remarks: "There were, it is true, in the middle colonies a few schools where *instruction of a more thorough*, if not of a more comprehensive, kind could be had *than is common now*. These schools were generally in charge of Scotch-Irish schoolmasters, whose success in imparting at least a thorough grammatical knowledge of the Latin language, and whose proficiency in the system they practiced in teaching the other branches, were plainly discernible in the career of many men who became prominent in the Revolution. Such was the school at New London, in Chester County, of which Dr. Allison, the famous Latinist, was head master, where George Reed, Benjamin Rush, Thomas McKean, Hugh Williamson, and John Ewing, amongst others, were educated. The system of these old schools was undoubtedly very narrow, so far as the mere acquisition of knowledge was concerned, but it had the inestimable advantage of training the pupils to think clearly and logically, and to cultivate the judgment." (Applause.)

Dr. Stillé further informs us, in relation to the education of John Dickinson himself, whose services during the Revolutionary period we all so well know and so highly appreciate, that all his early instruction, down to the time when he became a student of law in the office of his preceptor, was received from William Killen, a young Irishman, who at the age of fifteen years came to Dover, a homeless stranger, and was taken into the family of Mr. Dickinson's father. The same William Killen later became Chief Justice and Chancellor of the State of Delaware. (Applause.) It is to the influence of this youthful instructor that Dr. Stillé attributes, not only the early development of Mr. Dickinson's powers of thought and of action, but, also, his direct and forceful style of English composition and address. He was thus saved from the then prevailing Johnsonian pretentiousness and inflation of speech, and drilled to an expression of thought earnestly directed to the production of conviction and of deeds. Who ever heard of swelling and high-sounding periods from a Scotch-Irishman's pen? Such pretension and folly would belie and defeat the very end of his living.

Coming from a source, at once so authentic and impartial, the foregoing statements of fact and opinion lend a peculiar emphasis to the historic truth that the Scotch-Irish have made large and potent contributions to the educational influences of the country, and that they have left in this important field the same indelible mark of their intense and forceful natures which is to be found in almost every other field of human endeavor in the United States. (Applause.)

The evidence of this fact is, by no means, confined to the purely incidental allusions of Dr. Stillé, but is everywhere most abundant and striking, and deserves far more attention from this Society than it has yet received. This is neither the time nor the place for developing it, but the effect of some recent publications (laughter and applause) to cast a slur upon the intelligence, the education, and the conduct of the early Scotch-Irish settlers of the State, makes a present reference to it both timely and pertinent.

No race of all those whose united efforts and character has reared the noble fabric of our Commonwealth and Nation has contributed more to the educational development of the country than these very people who have sometimes been painted as ignorant and as riotous, as an uncouth and a disorderly class. Parallel with the movements of this race will generally be found the very best fruits of our educational life.

It would be well, indeed, in these days of extreme diffusiveness in our educational methods, when great caravansaries of learning, with their millions of endowment and vast corps of instructors, have supplanted the log colleges and Scotch-Irish academies, if we should occasionally turn our thoughts backward, ask after the characteristics of these early educators of the country, and compare the results of the two highly contrasted conditions. If I mistake not, the comparison would not always redound to the credit of our own day of academical wealth and extravagance. If it be true, as was asserted by Lord Chatham, "that for solidity of reasoning, force of sagacity, and wisdom of conclusion, under such a complication of difficult circumstances, no nation, or body of men, can stand in preference to the general Congress at Philadelphia," of 1775, there must somewhere be found the cause of such striking superiority. No one who studies the transactions of those days in comparison with the records of ancient or modern times can doubt the truth of Chatham's parliamentary declaration.

The causes of this greatness of mind and of purpose in our Revolutionary fathers are no doubt various, but the schoolmaster of the colonial days was not the least potent amongst them. There was nothing diffusive in his method of instruction. It was the very essence of concentration and intensity. He had himself received an early baptism of fire, and felt the impulse of a purpose which balked at no difficulties or privations. His personality was strong, his individuality distinct, and his aims always positive and direct. He bore an ardent hatred to all sophistry and pretense, never trifled with his own faculties, and never lapsed into a weak and useless dilettanteism.

The Scotch-Irish master had no monopoly of these high qualities, but they were his *par excellence* and above all others by virtue of his own hard training in a school specially devised by Providence for the production of men of tense and robust mental fibre, and he imparted them to his pupils with a vigor which awakened every latent faculty of the mind and implanted the fire of a holy purpose in the heart. It is thus alone that men can be made. No *useful* scholarship, indeed, can be nursed into being in the lap of luxury, or ground out by lifeless machinery in the schools, whatever may be their wealth of endowment or elaboration of appointment. There must be superadded to all this the inspiration of a high purpose and the discipline of severe thought, which nothing but the intense and stimulating personality of a strong man can supply. How often do we hear from our university graduates of the present day the plaintive cry that they never learned to think or to work, until that hard and wholesome lesson was taught them by the cruel necessities of their active life. How many of us have ourselves passed through a like experience, and been made to regret the absence of a training which no massive buildings, accumulated apparatus, or numerous corps of perfunctory instructors, ever did, or ever can, impart to the generous youth, in whose mind and heart lie infolded unknown potentialities of thought and purpose, which await but a proper inspiration and guidance to be awakened and directed into strong and beneficent activity. It is the great merit of those Scotch-Irish masters of the early days that they sent no pupil forth to reproach them in after years. They had trained the mind to vigorous thought, they had inspired in the heart a noble purpose, and thus opened the way for their pupils to all great achievement, in every field of human activity, to be limited only by their own natural endowments and the ordinary exigencies of practical life. No matter what fortune might hold in store for them, they held the priceless treasure of a character which no storm, or stress of adversity, could shake, or warp from the lines which had been set for it. To such men we, and the whole country, owe a debt of gratitude, which can be repaid in no other way than by transmitting their memories and their spirit to our posterity. Let us here record the debt and resolve that it shall be paid. (Applause.)

We have with us speakers whom I know you are all eager to hear, but before I take up the pleasant duty of presenting them to you, there are one or two announcements to be made concerning the present condition and recent work of the Association. During the past year there has been produced by one of our members, Rev. Dr. Henry C. McCook, an historical romance, "The Latimers," (applause), which I presume many of you have already read. Your Council thought they would be furthering the purpose of the Society to stimulate historical research concerning the Scotch-Irish in America, by an official recognition of this book in conformity with the intent of a resolution passed at one of your former meetings. They accordingly awarded to Dr. McCook the prize of $100, authorized by that resolution, for the best literary production on the Scotch-Irish in Pennsylvania, deemed worthy of being so crowned. (Applause.)

Dr. McCook, with that generosity of impulse which everywhere characterizes the Scotch-Irish race (laughter and applause), having accepted the proffered honor with many expressions of gratitude and appreciation, promptly returned the money to the Society's coffers, with a request that it be so used as to best promote the object of the award. (Applause.)

The volumes before you, as explained by the printed slip accompanying them, have been purchased with this fund, and are presented to you as a souvenir of this occasion, and of the generosity of the author. (Applause.)

The total present membership of the Society is about three hundred. There have been thirty new names added to the roll during the year just past. As the members have opportunity they will promote the interest and prosperity of the Society by presenting for membership the names of those who are worthy of such an honor, in their respective communities.

This, as you all perceive, is the most numerously attended of any of our banquets. The sudden accession of members, at the last moment, has necessitated a crowding which we regret, but he is no Scotch-Irishman who cannot rejoice even in adversity, when a feast like this is spread before him.

We have with us this evening a gentleman who has recently come from the scenes of war. (Applause.) This is always of interest to the Scotch-Irish people. (Laughter.) They love a fight, whenever it is a fight for principle; when it is an open fight, a frank fight, and a fight which does not carry with it rancor and enmity of heart. (Applause.) I am afraid that this gentleman is just now lying in wait for one of our friends. If the thunder which has been rumbling in my ear since he has been sitting here can be taken as a true indication of the impending storm, I would advise that particular guest to make sure his escape before the banquet adjourns. (Laughter.)

I now have the pleasure of introducing to you Senator Marcus A. Hanna, of Ohio. (Applause.)

Hon. Marcus A. Hanna :—

Mr. President and Gentlemen:—My presence here tonight is to be accounted for in two ways: The first, and most important, is that I did not see this programme until I got here. (Laughter.) I did not know that I was to be called upon under such embarrassing circumstances to make a speech. I will give Colonel Cassels just fifteen minutes to get out of the house. (Laughter.) However, now that I am here, and have met with such a hearty reception, which, from the nature of it, I know to be Scotch-Irish, I feel inclined to improve the opportunity offered me to thank the Society for the distinguished honor which it has conferred upon me in making me one of its members. (Applause.) I am reminded of the circumstance of my election by this beautiful souvenir which lies before me, from the pen of my dear friend and boyhood's schoolmate, the Rev. Henry C. McCook. (Applause.) I may be pardoned if I drop from the subject long enough to regret that he is not present with us to-night. (Cries of "He is here." Laughter and applause.)

Rev. Henry C. McCook :—

I have just got in. You are all right.

Hon. Marcus A. Hanna (continuing) :—

That little circumstance spoils my whole speech. Now that Dr. McCook is here I cannot say what I intended. But I am rather glad he is here, and he knows why—because he and I have been friends from the cradle. It was from him, and his companionship, that I had my first knowledge that I had Scotch-Irish blood in my veins. (Laughter.) I will tell you why—the remark of your Chairman has given me the opportunity. When Henry and I went to school together, we were companions; we were seatmates; we were chums. He was a better student than I, but I had more fun. (Laughter and applause.) It was part of our duty to our fellow schoolmates to have a scrap about three times a week. (Laughter.) Each of us walked around with a chip on our shoulders, and when it was said that one or the other had said that he could whip the other, it was immediately tried, and each was very earnest and anxious to begin—that was the Irish—and neither was ever ready to quit—and that was the Scotch. (Laughter and applause.)

The Scotch-Irish blood has made us such dear friends and kindred spirits, that he has been fighting the devil and I have been fighting Democrats ever since. (Laughter and applause.)

Henry found out, somehow, that I am of Scotch-Irish stock—— (Laughter and applause.) How do you suppose I am going to make a speech? (Laughter.) So when he notified me of this fact, and that after a thorough investigation of my record, he had found me eligible for membership in this distinguished Society, and asked the privilege of presenting my name, I consented with alacrity, because wherever I have known a Scotch-Irishman I have always found a good fellow. I wish to take this opportunity to express my gratification that he took the trouble to find me out and bring me before the public. (Laughter and applause.) If he had not known that I was a Scotch-Irishman I do not think I would have had any notoriety in this country. (Laughter.)

The pleasant thing to me about such reunions as these is that I am never called upon to make a speech; that I always meet a lot of jolly good fellows, and have a good time. This is not an exception to the rule. Therefore, gentlemen, notwithstanding my embarrassment in not having made any preparation to entertain you, I am glad that I came, and I make the promise that I will continue to come as long as I am able to make the point of rendezvous.

Now, gentlemen, there is no use, after so much hilarity, of my trying to strike a sentimental mood, for I cannot get on in that way, and therefore can only repeat what I have said, that I feel more than satisfied with my connection with this Society, and more than gratified to have met you all. I hope that the opportunity for a reunion will come to me for many years, and that I will be taken into full communion here, and into the hearts of the Scotch-Irish, which are always in the right place. (Laughter and applause.)

The President :—

I see that Dr. McCook is now present with us. He is Chairman of the Committee on History and Archives. I will call upon him for his report, as such Chairman, before presenting to you our next scheduled speaker. (Applause.)

Rev. Henry C. McCook, D. D. :—

GENTLEMEN:—One of the subjects of the Historical Report of last year, I am happy to say, is here—our distinguished friend, Mr. Hanna. His name "bewrayeth" him. I wonder he did not understand long ago that all the Hannas are either Scotch or Scotch-Irish. But the hot blood of Ulster is so gently tempered with the sweet savour of his Quaker parentage that it was not until the last presidential campaign put him on the warpath that the "true inwardness" of his ancestral blood was made outwardly manifest.

It is certainly an historical peculiarity that we have a "Fisher" presiding on this occasion at our banquet. I am sure he will do full justice to the subjects that will be presented from time to time, and I am glad that, even with Judge Stewart in the room, he has had such a cordial reception from the guests. (Laughter.) However, it is needless to explain that he is not "Mr. Sidney George Fisher."

Whatever we may say or think about what has been said or what has not been said concerning the Scotch-Irish in Pennsylvania, there is at least one historian who, in his last work, "Virginia and Her Neighbors," has done full justice to the Scotch-Irish in the few remarks he has made towards the close of that admirable history. I refer to the eminent historian, John Fisk. I venture to call your attention to the fact that he has promised in his next history to treat of Pennsylvania, and we may confidently anticipate a book well worth reading, and moreover one that in all respects will be just to the Scotch-Irish. We are not expecting plaudits alone; we do not claim that our forebears were perfect. But we have a right to ask that a historian shall deal with judicial fairness and truthfulness with their sturdy merits, and not present their actions, whether good or evil, in a distorting light.

I will not detain you with a long report this evening. You will remember that Professor Thompson was not willing to concede the fact that the Scotch-Irish, among their various achievements in this country, had developed a poet. It is just possible that he proved his point. At all events there is one ballad which has a historic place among the Scotch-Irish— "The Ballad of Boyne Water." Is an extremely interesting if not a highly poetic composition. It is a misfortune perhaps that it was long considered a sort of badge of a particular form of religion, in fact, an Ulster Protestant song. It is a Protestant song undoubtedly, and owed its great popularity to that fact. But we are not disposed now, so far as we are Scotch-Irishmen, to be either Protestant or Roman Catholic. We are simply considering the quaint old ballad in the historic spirit. Of course, we are proud to feel that all the history of this country belong to us. (Laughter.) Oh, I am not claiming that we made it all—not quite! But all is ours to possess and enjoy. I do not think that while we claim for our fathers their deserts, we are so narrow and unjust as to refuse to others that which is their due. I dare say we will admit that occasionally there has been a little overstatement of the achievements of our ancestors. (Laughter.) Possibly that was due to our close affiliation with our

New England friends. (Renewed laughter.) We have been compelled, as it were, to emphasize the fact that here we are, and that we have been here all along. If it had not been for that fact, which was not so much an exaggeration of the actual state of things as an undue emphasis, the historians, of whatever ilk, would not have found out that Scotch-Irishmen have been in America from the beginning helping to make the history of the country. Very well, now that they have found us out, we can afford to be a little more modest, thus reverting to the original and natural Irish temperament. (Laughter.)

To return to the Ballad of the Boyne Water, which we are to consider not from a controversial, but from an historical standpoint. There are two versions, and I have found both of them in America. I was much interested in finding an old gentleman—a Mr. Roney, of Scotch-Irish descent. (Laughter and applause, provoked by the pending political contest over Mr. Roney for Collector of Taxes.) Gentlemen, if you have read "The Latimers" you have found out that the Scotch-Irish are not very kindly disposed towards taxes or tax collectors, and I have no reference one way or another to the Roney who is now so manifest on the political horizon. (Laughter.) I was gratified to find, in asking the worthy gentleman, Mr. George D. Roney, to whom I have alluded, concerning his recollection of the Boyne Water, that he was able to give at least one verse of what is considered to be the original version. It is an interesting fact that this old form was planted in America alongside of what is the popular version, for Mr. Roney is American-born. This is the verse which the venerable gentleman recited to me, and which, as you will presently see, corresponds with the earliest version of the ballad:—

"July the first, one morning clear,
One thousand six hundred and ninety,
King William did his men prepare,
For thousand he had thirty,
To meet King James and all his hosts
In camp near the Boyne Water."

The popular version of the ballad I now give as dictated from memory by an aged Scotch-Irish aunt, Aunt Fanny McCook:—

THE BALLAD OF BOYNE WATER.

I.

July the first, near old Bridgetown,
    There was a grievi—ous battle,
Where many a man lay on the plain
    By cannons that did rattle.
King James he pitched his tent between
    The lines for to reti—re,
But William threw his bomb balls in
    And set them all on fi—re.

II.

With threat and rage they vowed revenge
    Upon King William's forces,
And oft would cry out veh'mently
    That they would stop his courses.
A bullet from the Irish came,
    That grazed King William's ar—m,
They tho't his majesty was slain,
    But it did him little har—m.

III.

Duke Schoemberg then with friendly care
    His king would often caution
To shun the spot where bullets hot
    Retained their rapid motion;
But William said, "He don't deserve
    The name of Faith's Defender,
Who would not venture life and limb
    To make a foe surrender."

IV.

And we the Boyne began to cross,
    The enemy they descended;
But few of our brave men were lost,
    For stoutly we defended.
The horse were the first that marchèd o'er,
    The trot soon followed after;
But brave Duke Schoemberg was no more,
    By venturing over the water.

V.

When valiant Schoemberg he was slain,
    Our King he then accosted
His warlike men for to march on,
    And he would be the foremost.
"Brave boys," he said, " be not dismayed,
    For losing one commander;
For God will be our King this day
    And I'll be general under!"

VI.

Then stoutly we the Boyne did cross
    To give our enemies battle;
Our cannons, to our foe's great cost,
    Like thundering claps did rattle.
Majestic mien our Prince rode o'er;
    His men soon followed after,
With blows and shout put our foes to rout
    The day we crossed the water.

VII.

The Protestants of Drogheda
    Have reason to be thankful,
That they were not to bondage bro't,
    Be—ing but a handful.
First to the towncil they were brought,
    And tried at Millmount after;
But brave King William set them free,
    By venturing over the water.

VIII.

The cunning French near to Dunleith
    Had taken up their quarters,
And fenced themselves on every side
    Still waiting for new orders.
But in the dead time of the night
    They set the fields on fi—re,
And long before the morning light
    To Dublin did reti—re.

IX.

Then said King William to his men
    After the French departed;
"I'm glad," said he, "that none of ye
    Seem—ed to be faint hearted.
So sheath your swords and rest awhile;
    In time we'll follow after."
These words he uttered with a smile
    The day we crossed the water.

X.

> Come, let us all with heart and voice
> Laud our lives' defender,
> Who at the Boyne his valour showed,
> And made his foes surrender.
> To Him above the praise we'll give
> Both now and ever after;
> And bless the glorious memory
> Of William that crossed the Boyne Water.

Mr. Pollock :—

We have a little matter at this end of the table. I am about to introduce an ex-President of the Society, who is the representative of the honest dollar in Pennsylvania, and is now engaged in the spoon business—the Hon. C. Stuart Patterson. (Applause.)

Hon. C. Stuart Patterson :—

MR. PRESIDENT AND GENTLEMEN OF THE SOCIETY:—I have a pleasant duty to perform. There are pleasures in life, and there are duties in life, but it does not always happen that the pleasures are duties, nor that the duties are pleasant; but upon this particular occasion the duty which I have to perform is an exceedingly pleasant one. I am charged by the Society, Mr. President, as an expression of its gratification with your admirable administration, to present to you a tribute of its regard.

I may be permitted to say that, as my eye rests upon the Senatorial guest of honor, I am reminded of a story, which has also been recalled to my mind by the references, made by the gentleman who has just taken his seat, to his Quaker ancestry. I am reminded of a wedding in Pennsylvania, in the early days, in the Society of Friends, when, after the two contracting parties had made their solemn declarations to the assembled Society, the presiding elder said: "Is there anybody here who has any objections to make?" One man arose instantly in the end of the hall, and said: "Yes; I have an objection of a serious character to make. I had reserved Hannah for myself." (Laughter and applause.) The State of Ohio is somewhat more fortunate than the objector was upon that occasion. The State of Ohio has reserved Hanna for herself, and has succeeded, fortunately, not only for that State, but fortunately, also, for the whole country (great applause), in returning Mr. Hanna to that place in the councils of the nation which he ought to occupy. (Applause.)

Mr. President, the Society presents to you this spoon, not because you are regarded as a stirrer up of strife, but because it has occurred to the Society that so distinguished a representative of its principles will hereafter continue to live up to those principles, and that from this time forward you will, as becomes all ex-Presidents of this Society, abjure terrapin and canvas-back ducks, and all other things that carnal minds and bodies are wont to indulge in, and that you will confine yourself to that porridge, which, together with the Shorter Catechism, represents (laughter) that low living and high thinking, which are the embodiment of true Scotch-Irish principles.

Mr. President, the proposition to present this tribute to you was received by the Society with almost absolute unanimity, but I am obliged, in the truth of history, to say that when I said to Judge Stewart, "We propose to give Fisher a spoon," he looked at me with his glittering eyes and said solemnly, "When I shall have finished with Mr. Fisher to-night there will not be enough of him left to present anything to." (Laughter and applause.) But when I explained to him that the gentleman whom this Society proposed to honor is not the historian, who has written those fascinating novels, but is the gentleman who has maintained the honor and the dignity of this Society for the past year, he at once gave his most cordial and most willing assent.

Mr. President, it is right that I should call your attention to certain features which are symbolized in the gift.

In the first place, you will observe the head of the Aborigine upon the top of the spoon. That has solved an ethnological difficulty which has puzzled some people. You know there are good Indians, and there are bad Indians, just as there are good people of various sorts, and bad people; and you know that as a general rule the bad people are people who are not Scotch-Irishmen, and the good people are Scotch-Irishmen. (Laughter.) And when you look at this sculptured Indian here you will discover that beyond the shadow of a doubt he was himself a good Indian, and, therefore, a Scotch-Irishman. (Laughter.) That establishes the universal predominance of our race.

Of course, there are the other emblems here which represent the history of our race; and I might go through them one after another, but there is one emblem to which I want particularly to direct your attention, and that is this, that the prominent feature of this spoon is the presence of its backbone. That is the distinguishing peculiarity of the Scotch-Irish race. (Laughter.) Whenever you put a Scotch-Irishman in the front of anything he is there to stay. Whenever you put him in the command of an advance position, and leave him there, you may be perfectly certain that when you come back that advanced position will have been moved forward, or he will be dead. (Laughter and applause.) Whenever you put a Scotch-Irishman at the head of any principle, whether in Church or State, you may be perfectly certain that that principle will march to victory. I beg to say, sir, that there never was a time in the history of this country when the presence of a backbone in men in public life was more important than at this precise moment. (Applause.) The President of the United States has struck the key note for us. (Applause.) We do not intend to let our enemies dictate our line of battle. We intend to march forward; and we intend that those results that were not partisan, but were and are for the good of the whole country, and which were accomplished in the election of 1896, shall not be lost now. (Applause.) I beg to say to the gentlemen in Washington that they may play their game of politics, but the people of the United States have resolved that the contest shall go on until the credit of the United States shall be securely established at the highest point among the nations of the world, there to remain. (Applause.)

I have the great satisfaction, sir, upon behalf of this Society, of presenting to you this tribute, which very feebly indicates the affection and the regard which the Society justly entertains for you. (Applause and cries of "Good.")

The President :—

GENTLEMEN OF THE SCOTCH-IRISH SOCIETY:—It is with unqualified pleasure and appreciation that I accept this exquisite and significant token, not indeed as a personal tribute to myself—I wish I could feel that I merited such an expression of your regard—I accept it as a tribute to the office with which you have honored me. There is nothing I should cherish more deeply—there is nothing which would lend greater encouragement and inspiration to my life than to feel that I had and deserved the affection, the confidence, the lasting friendship and support of the body of men who assemble here from year to year. (Applause.) In the sterling qualities of the genuine Scotch-Irishman, as symbolized by this spoon, I firmly believe. I do not know whether my friend, Dr. McCook, has yet learned the lesson—he seems to have doubted its truth—but I believe also in Scotch-Irish modesty. (Laughter.) Modesty and strength everywhere go hand in hand. The true Scotch-Irishman is generous and brave, he is modest and strong, and these are qualities which give value to friendship. We fight fiercely, indeed, and with a boldness which never blenches, but it is only as we are driven thereto by conviction. It is never with rancor.

There have never been more pleasant scenes about this board than when the men of the South and the men of the North have mingled here in friendly banter—men who fought with unflinching and equal bravery on the opposite sides of a deadly conflict. They met here as brothers. They met with entire respect for each other. Neither would have yielded his principles to fear or to force, but the battle concluded, like brave men, they take counsel together for the commonweal. Such are the men we love. Such the men whose friendship we cherish. (Applause.)

We have with us to-night a distinguished representative of one of the educational institutions of this State, which preserves the spirit and tone of the Scotch-Irish influence to which it owes its existence. He is a clergyman, and can ——

Dr. Warfield (interrupting) :—
No; no.

The President:—

I beg Dr. Warfield's pardon. (Laughter.) I thought he could enlighten us on the Scotch-Irish creed, and had actually picked up a text for his use. Since the cloth is disclaimed, I shall leave him to carve out a road for himself.

I now have the pleasure of presenting to you Dr. Ethelbert D. Warfield, President of Lafayette College. (Applause.)

President Ethelbert D. Warfield, LL. D. :—

MR. PRESIDENT AND FELLOW SCOTCH-IRISHMEN:—I really should like to have my ecclesiastical *status* settled. I have had great difficulty ever since I became President of Lafayette College in determining whether I am a preacher or not. My good friend who sits at the head of the table is responsible, I believe, for this confusion. Immediately upon my election he invited me to fill the pulpit of his church during the following Summer, and though I declined, his example proved irresistible until a few weeks ago I found that I was about to be shut out of Girard College because I bore a better reputation in the city of Philadelphia than I deserved. (Laughter.)

I do not know whether the late Mr. Daniel Tucker was a Scotch-Irishman or not. It seems to me that almost every other person celebrated in song or story has been claimed for that race. Certainly it seems that I have adopted him for my patron saint. And for a hungry man who has just come off the train after a long journey to be given this *menu* card and only asked to make a speech, there is small satisfaction unless it can be proved that he is to go down to posterity in connection with some gentlemen of literary distinction. As our friend, Mr. Hanna, has suggested, "literary fellows" have no standing in politics, and the Scotch-Irish poet is yet to be born. But the true Scotch-Irishman pants and yearns after the rewards of learning.

Who are these Scotch-Irishmen, anyhow? What is the test that is to be applied to them? I observed in the volume of the proceedings of the first Scotch-Irish congress that nearly all the distinguished men of our Revolutionary epoch were claimed for the race. There was Patrick Henry and

Thomas Jefferson, James Madison and John Marshall, John Witherspoon and Paul Jones, and a variety of other persons of more or less varied descent and vigorous dissent. Now, if these gentlemen had been seeking entry by their pedigrees into any such register as the Shorthorn Herd-Book, upon which I was trained up, they would not have been eligible for entry as thoroughbreds. One drop of Scotch-Irish blood, however, seems to be that "one touch of nature which makes the whole world kin." If any refinement upon this standard is admitted, it seems to be a smattering of the Shorter Catechism.

This catechism test I believe to be a sound one. My little boy, who is just six years old, makes a very decided distinction in the Sunday afternoon discussions upon questions of divinity. He never debates a Shorter Catechism question with his Scotch-Irish father, but he is a ready conversationalist with his Puritan mother. I inquired recently why this was, and his reply was: "Well, you don't ask me these questions out of a book, but mamma does, and I want to see whether she really knows them or not." (Laughter.)

Now, that is the difference between the New England Puritan and the Scotch-Irish Presbyterian in practical mastery of polemical piety.

I was pleased to learn a moment ago that a certificate had been granted to a Scotch-Irish professor as the true fountain head of English, pure and undefiled, in these United States. I have long believed that the best English was good Scotch, nor do I think that the converse of that proposition ought to be doubted. But when I married a New England wife I found that it was at least open to debate. For a family altar was immediately erected in our home, and to my surprise it consisted of an unabridged dictionary instead of a Shorter Catechism. It is needless to say that though I have been daily sacrificed upon that altar, I have my own opinion still, although I express that opinion with the usual modesty of the Scotch-Irishman. (Laughter and applause.)

It is very easy to see the Scotch-Irish element in Philadelphia. When I speak at a Philadelphia dinner I always look with anxiety to see whether I am to speak early or late in the programme, for I have observed that owing to the retiring character of the Scotch-Irish element those who speak late are likely to have their discourse largely to themselves. Although I have cast some reflections upon the pedigrees of the typical Scotch-Irishman in American history, I believe I am entitled myself to registry. I think I know my ropes, and can distinguish the times when they are something to hang to and to hang with. It is said that there is a race which scarcely finds it safe to trace its pedigree very far in the past lest it come to an ancestor whose acquaintance with the cord was more cordial than accordant with the purposes of heraldry. But the Scotch-Irishman is rarely at the end of his rope, but if he is it is likely to be the right end. If I may give you an historical example I will point my moral with a page of family history. We are interested, with that humility which is a Scotch-Irish trait, in the dashing deeds of our ancestor, Gen. William Campbell, who performed so notable an exploit in 1780, at the battle of King's Mountain. The Irish gentleman, Major Patrick Ferguson, who had established himself upon that height, learned the value of the Scotch infusion when Campbell and his mountaineers swept down from their eyrie and closed his career and opened the campaign of Yorktown. A little earlier than this Colonel (for such he then was) Campbell was charged with the agreeable duty, for the Scotch-Irishman always finds his duty pleasant, of keeping down the Tories. One Sabbath morning while riding home from church with his wife on a pillion behind him, in the homely fashion of that simple day, he saw a notorious Tory, who had recently escaped from jail, dash across the road and disappear in the forest. Telling his wife to jump down, he gave chase and presently overtook the Tory and captured him in the neighboring river. Leading him out of the water, after a brief consultation he hung him to a tree with the straps of the pillion. Riding back to where he had left his wife, she said to him, "Well, Mr. Campbell, what did you do?" He replied, "Why, I caught him, Betsy." "Well, what did you do to him?" "Why, I hung him, Betsy." "Well, ——" said Mrs. Campbell; but he interrupted her, saying, "But, my dear, we'll not discuss secular matters on the

Sabbath day." My *alter ego*, Dry-as-dust the Historian, repudiates this last remark as not in the sources. So much the worse for the sources, say I. Thus he illustrated a distinguishing characteristic of the Scotch-Irishman. He knew just how far his duty required him to go and just where a painful duty became a pleasant diversion.

Yet even a Scotch-Irishman has sometimes found it impossible to resist an inclination to be over-impetuous. Perhaps it sprang up in an otherwise placid people as a natural reaction from association with the Quaker on the one hand and the Pennsylvania German on the other. I remember when I was a boy that there was a long drought in Kentucky. My grandfather Breckinridge, who, as a typical Scotch-Irishman, believed in Providence, and in a Providence which provided what was best for the people, long resisted the importunity of his people to pray for rain. But when July had passed and August had come, and neither the former nor the latter rain had fallen upon the earth, a committee waited upon him and said: "Dr. Breckinridge, you must pray for rain." "Well," he replied, "I think the Lord knows His own business and I don't like to dictate to Him; but if you insist I will pray for rain." That morning, in the course of his long prayer, which is those days was no misnomer, he prayed, as only a Scotch-Irishman can pray, for an outpouring of the waters of Heaven. The unwily congregation remained for an old-fashioned Presbyterian sermon, but before it was done the wind arose and the rain descended, the roof of the church was blown off—and a soaking congregation returned home consoling themselves with the thought that the ground was as wet as they. But the situation was too much for one ancient parishioner who made the personal complaint: "Now, that is just the way with you, Dr. Breckinridge; you never know how to do a thing like that in moderation." (Laughter and applause.)

But there is a very deep side to these Scotch-Irish traits. I realize that such an ancestry as ours is a precious possession, because it stands for some of the supremest things in the world. Dean Swift long ago spoke of

"The two noblest things, which are sweetness and light."

Our age has taken up and echoed the phrase and Matthew Arnold has refashioned it as one of the shibboleths of contemporary culture. But the Scotch-Irishman, both in word and life, phrased his ideals yet more gloriously. He spoke of "the two noblest things, which are faith and frugality." These accordant ideals have not only made the Scotch-Irishmen what they are, but they are able to make for any race and any land a gracious history. (Applause.)

The President of this Society in his introductory remarks spoke of the log school house in which the early academies of our people had their early beginnings. Out of these log school houses there came forth many who were trained to frugal living and lofty faith. It has been the glory of the Presbyterian Church not so much that it has always insisted upon an educated ministry, but that it has equally insisted upon the necessity of an educated laity; a laity and a clergy learned not only in the learning of this world, but also able to give a reason for the faith that is in them. (Applause.)

It is a familiar thing to hear the school house of New England spoken of as the cornerstone of American liberty. But there is a Scotch-Irish institution more universal and more influential among us than the little red school house of the New England village. For even where, upon the extremest confines of civilization, it was impossible for the log school house and the wandering *dominie* to penetrate, there was that dearest and most devoted of influences, the Scotch-Irish mother, and at that mother's knee the children learned not only their letters and how to read, out of the dear old Bible, but learned also to stand face to face with God. (Applause.) They too were taught, ere they could speak their mother language plain, the noble words of our dear old catechism, and had impressed upon them that simple yet sublime philosophy which is summed up in the answer to its first question: "Man's chief end is to glorify God and enjoy Him forever." From their youth they learned that there are influences in life which are beyond the circumstances of earth, and it gave to them an expectation of the future which not only cheered and strengthened them in adversity, but gave them an eagerness of vision and a serenity of heart which led them to make for themselves new homes in the wilderness, broad ways for the advance of civilization on earth, and straight paths towards their assured entrance into eternal life. (Applause.)

Though I draw my paternal descent and name from the Puritans of Maryland, that little colony that found a shelter beneath the rule of exiled Romanists from the persecution of their fellow-Protestants of Virginia, I rejoice that it has been again and again intermingled with the blood of Pennsylvania and Virginia Scotch-Irishmen; blood of the Caldwells, Sutherlands, Breckinridges, Prestons, Buchanans, and Campbells—all of them men who never faltered in their faith in God or the purpose which they were assured that God had for this dear land of ours.

In this day, when we are under the shadow of many doubts and fears, when corruption at home and treachery abroad seem to threaten the fair name of the Republic, we may well lift a prayer to Him who rules in the army of Heaven and among the inhabitants of the earth that He will awaken again in our midst the old faith and spread abroad the old frugality, that our men may be as the men of old, strong, confident, and self-restrained. In that day the trumpet gave no uncertain sound in the day of battle. Men fought not as self-seekers, but that the cause of God might triumph. Ours is an imperial land to-day; it has increased and multiplied and possessed the continent. The prayers of the fathers have been answered; the expectation of their hearts has been realized; the heritage which they sought has been transmitted to us. We may well glory in our country and our civilization, but let us not forget to join with joyous hearts in the noble prayer of the old version of the Psalms:—

> "God of our fathers, be the God
> Of their succeding race."

(Great applause.)

The President :—

I think you will all excuse my mistake as to Dr. Warfield's profession. If he is not a preacher he ought to have been one. He would have adorned the desk and expounded sound doctrine to the saints. (Applause.)

There is no sphere in our civic life where the Scotch-Irish character has left a deeper impress than upon the judicial and legal institutions of this State. We are all familiar with the names of the great Chief Justices, McKean, and Gibson, and Black, and other distinguished jurists of the blood, who have dignified and adorned the bench of the past. The line, we are happy to think, is still perpetuated by those in all ways worthy of the succession to so grave a trust and so arduous a duty. The administration of the laws is safe in their hands.

I now have the pleasure of introducing to you as our next speaker, the Hon. John B. McPherson, of the Court of Common Pleas of Dauphin County, who will speak upon the judiciary of the Commonwealth. (Applause.)

Hon. John B. McPherson:—

I trust the Society will permit me to depart from the usual course on such occasions, and to treat the subject just named by the President in a short paper instead of an address. When the Council did me the honor to suggest this topic, the temptation assailed me to choose the short and easy method. It did not seem difficult to outline a more or less eloquent oration, which might perhaps begin by dwelling with some rhetorical emphasis on the abounding and eminent virtues of our unobtrusive race, and might then go on to point out (perhaps superfluously) that when a Scotch-Irishman and a position of honor or emolument come into reasonable proximity, the one will inevitably assimilate the other. An allusion would naturally follow to Chief Justices Gibson and Black; a few other names redolent of Ulster might be mentioned here and there; and, the peroration being now happily in sight, the end might be fittingly reached by referring in a laudatory strain to their numerous brethren and fellow-countrymen, living as well as dead, who have strongly influenced the development, &c., &c., and in this and every other direction have left their impress, &c., &c.

But I seemed to foresee, that after the very moderate applause had died away neither the speaker nor his audience would be the richer by a definite fact or a definite idea upon a subject that deserves a more serious treatment. I determined therefore to accept the assignment in a prosaic spirit, and try to gather some facts instead of relying upon mere impressions and a general, unverified estimate. I hasten to add that you need not dread to be wearied with names and dates in detail; an appendix will contain the necessary lists, which I shall not read now, and you need not read at your convenience. The time at my command was so limited that I have been able to do little in comparison with what should be done, and will be done I hope by some gentleman of leisure in search of an occupation. Much information has been obtained by correspondence, and much has been gathered from official records, local histories, and biographical sketches, and from the extensive knowledge of two or three antiquarians who were kind enough to give me aid. No doubt there are mistakes and omissions, but on the whole I believe the conclusions reached to be fairly accurate.

The oldest book on the shelves of the Secretary of the Commonwealth that contains a record of commissions and appointments to the office of judge begins with the Revolution. The names of these officials during the provincial period may be found in the third and ninth volumes of the Pennsylvania Archives, second series; but for the sake of completeness the roll of the Supreme Court of the Province accompanies the lists of the later judges. As you no doubt know, there was originally no requirement in Pennsylvania that a judge of any court should be learned in the law. It was not until 1791 that an express command on this subject appears, and then it is only applied to the judges of the lower courts. It may not be so generally known that a similar provision concerning the justices of the Supreme Court was not put upon the statute-book until forty years more had gone by. As far as I can discover, the revised Act of 1834 contains the first express requirement that they shall be of professional learning. The third section enjoins that any vacancy thereafter occurring on the supreme bench shall be filled by a person not only of known integrity and ability—this being the phrase previously used to describe the necessary qualifications—but also of skill in the laws. In the lower courts I have confined my inquiries to the period from 1791 forward, but have included in the roll of the Supreme Court all the justices from the time of the Revolution. The lists that lie before me therefore contain the names of the Pennsylvania judiciary for more than a century, arranged according to the courts and counties in which they served. I have felt justified by the history of the Scotch-Irish name in admitting Scotsmen also to the roll, whether born in Scotland and coming directly here, or born in this country of ancestors that had not lived in Ireland, especially when the change of allegiance was several generations old. I have therefore counted among the Ulstermen the few judges that are thus more immediately Scottish, such as Justices Brackenridge and Burnside of the Supreme Court, and Judges Addison and Bird Wilson of the Common Pleas.

The results of the inquiry may be stated in a few words. There have been fifty-four justices of the Supreme Court since the Revolution, of whom thirty (including five Scotsmen) come of our blood. In their ranks are numbered nine of the sixteen chief justices and four members of the present court. The recently created Superior Court contains three judges eligible to membership in this Society. On the bench of the Common Pleas and Orphans' Court, judges belonging to this stock have presided in every county of the Commonwealth, except Lackawanna, Sullivan, and Wyoming; and in two of these, judges of Scottish descent have a place upon the register. Sullivan is the single county that adds no name to the catalogue; but concerning the ancestry of three of its ten judges I could learn nothing whatever. As might be expected, the proportion varies in different parts of the State. In the communities about Philadelphia and along the course of the Delaware, in the Wyoming Valley and near the New York border, the English and New England influence has been large; while the German settlers in Berks, Lehigh, Schuylkill, and the neighboring counties have contributed numerously to the list in that region. Nevertheless the Scotch-Irishman is by no means absent from these sections of the Commonwealth, although in the days when judges were appointed he sometimes came from a county outside the district. This method of selection, however, passed away in 1851, so that for nearly half the period under consideration the judges have been elected, and with rare exceptions have been chosen from the resident bar. Along the northern tier it may be noted that of the twenty-three judges who have presided in Susquehanna, Bradford, Tioga, McKean, and Potter, twelve have been Scotch-Irish, the ancestry of two of the other eleven being unknown; and seven of the seventeen (four of these being still in doubt) who served in the courts of Erie and Warren. The counties of Berks, Lancaster, Lehigh, Northampton, Schuylkill, and Lebanon, which are largely German in composition, have had sixty-one judges, but twenty-five of them have been of our line, and five have not yet been assigned. Of the three "home counties," Bucks has had two Scotsmen and four of Scotch-Irish strain among her thirteen judges; Chester, eight (one being Scottish) among fifteen; and Philadelphia, so far as I have been able to ascertain, twenty-two (three being Scotsmen) among eighty-seven. Of the Philadelphia judges, however, I have no information concerning more than half, but I believe the large majority of these are of English or other than Scotch-Irish ancestry. As a shining example of the perseverance of the saints, it may be observed that the president judges now in commission in Chester and Bucks, and eleven out of Philadelphia's sixteen judges would be qualified for admission into our ranks, if the Scottish extraction of three among the eleven is reckoned as equivalent to Ulster descent.

After the Susquehanna has been crossed, the tracks of the Scotch-Irish migration are easy to follow. Indeed, they cannot be avoided, for they are broad and well marked in every county west of the river and south of the northern tier. In five counties—Juniata, Perry, Fulton, Butler, and Lawrence—the bench has been solidly Scotch-Irish. In ten others—Mifflin, Blair, Armstrong, Clarion, Westmoreland, Greene, Cameron, Franklin, Fulton, and Beaver—there has been one exception; while in eleven—Cumberland, Bedford, Somerset, Union, Snyder, Mercer, Jefferson, Washington, Fayette, Forest, and Indiana—the exceptions are only two, and in Adams and Huntingdon only three. In the remaining counties of this region the division has been more nearly equal; but, be the majority large or small, it remains true that on every judicial roll in this great section of the Commonwealth, except in Lycoming, Elk, and Crawford, there is a majority of some size in favor of the Ulstermen. In Lycoming, they may claim four out of ten, and in Crawford six out of fifteen, the ancestry of four being unascertained; while in Elk the proportion is three to four, with one not yet assigned. In Allegheny the list shows the Scotch-Irish to outnumber the others more than two to one, ten of the eleven judges now upon the bench being of this lineage. If the present judges in the region under consideration are alone considered, only nine out of the forty-five are without this strain in their blood; and if the whole State to-day is taken into the account, sixty-two of the Common Pleas and Orphans' Court judges now in office trace some line of their ancestry to Ulster or Scotland, thirty-three to other countries, while concerning five no information has been obtained.

In brief, there have been three hundred and seventy-six judges of the Common Pleas or Orphans' Court in Pennsylvania since 1791. Of this number one hundred and ninety, or two more than fifty per cent. of the whole, belong to our stock in some degree; one hundred and nineteen belong to other families, while the ancestry of sixty-seven is still undetermined. Doubtless in this latter class some Scotch-Irishmen are still to be found; but as forty-five of the number were on the bench of Philadelphia County, it is probable that few remain to be reclaimed. Adding the justices of the Supreme and Superior Courts that have not already been counted while in the Common Pleas, brings the number of judges learned in the law since the Revolution to four hundred and thirty-eight. Of this number, two hundred and twenty-three, or slightly more than one-half, are Scottish or Scotch-Irish in some degree, one hundred and thirty-nine belong to other nationalities and countries, and of sixty-nine no information, or no satisfactory information, has yet been obtained. If any one objects to the inclusion of Scotsmen in these lists, the number to be deducted does not exceed fourteen.

This survey is incomplete in two directions. The ancestry

of eighty persons remains to be investigated; neither has any effort been made to estimate the value of the services rendered by those whom we may properly reckon among our kinsmen. I hope the latter defect at least may be made good by some competent hand. But as the task calls for careful study of the work done by each man in its relation to the social, political, and legal development of the Commonwealth, the results would be scarcely suitable for post-prandial consumption.

The facts I have given speak with their own emphasis concerning the stock from which we spring, and I shall add little by way of comment. But this much at least should be said: They are not brought forward in a spirit of rivalry with other nationalities, nor in any temper of extravagant eulogy. In these lists are many names that belong to us in part, but not exclusively. Our sister societies might claim them also with an equal right, and sometimes with a much better title. Moreover, a similar claim would be quite as valid upon many of ourselves. Few around this table are of pure Ulster descent, and no doubt many owe much to other strains; but even if our blood were still unmixed, we should honor no less highly our friends and neighbors from other lands and of other families. Nothing is further from our thoughts than to disparage their deeds or even seem to undervalue their admirable qualities. Our aim is simply to gather the facts concerning one famous stock among others, and to rescue from undeserved obscurity the story of its doings. When this has been done for ourselves, and done also for our English and German, our Irish and Welsh and Huguenot friends, each will be the richer for sharing the just pride of the other, while each in turn recounts its contribution to the common heritage of American achievement. (Applause.)

This also I think may be fairly urged: Whatever else may have contributed to the success of the Scotch-Irishman in the particular field now under consideration, he certainly owes much to his religious creed. It has lately grown somewhat into fashion to assert that Calvinism is a system of which the world is weary; and no doubt its uncompromising demands are not in favor with those that are unacquainted with its mighty spirit. I have no wish now to dispute the assertion; it might be pertinent to reply that Calvinism shows little sign of having grown so weary of the world as to be on the point of loosing its tenacious hold; but I simply wish to recall to your minds that this form of doctrine has had a peculiar attraction for the strongest races of the modern world. It is the sternest of creeds, but it does not crush; on the contrary, it nourishes as no other creed has ever nourished a passion for justice, a sense of individual dignity, and a supreme love of liberty. Where else in the history of belief can be found such absolute surrender to the sternest idea of justice—so absolute, indeed, that God himself does not escape from its demands, and the offender can never hope for pardon until his consciousness of violated law and inexorable penalty has forced him to the lowest deep of shame and confession? What other system has so exalted the divine sovereignty, that to one who feels himself upborne by this tremendous thought all distinctions between mere men fade into nothingness, and the oppression of one man by his fellow becomes unbearable arrogance, because it is seen to be not only a violation of personal freedom, but a usurpation and abuse of the divine prerogative? What other system of belief, in the same measure as this, sets the individual man face to face with his Creator, shuts out the rest of the universe from that awful interview, and compels him unaided to make his peace with an offended God? With all this, can there be found elsewhere so lofty an estimate of individual worth, such insistence on the divine within each man's soul, such emphasis on his single fate as the absorbing topic of the universe, so unyielding and yet so uplifting a demand that he shall never fail to conform to a splendid, and all the more splendid because a consciously impossible, standard? It is true that Calvinism is not milk for babes; even for adolescent races it may lack somewhat in nourishing quality; but for the strong it has been meat on which millions have thriven mightily and done great deeds for mankind. Even its great paradox has presented little difficulty to its true adherents; they *know* that God's foreordaining power and man's free will do co-exist as necessary truths of Christian consciousness, and with the Saxon contempt of formal logic they pay small heed to the violated syllogism. It is not from the followers of Calvin that the ranks of fatalism are recruited.

Born and bred in this creed under its various denominational names; sprung from the stock whose capacities and virtues I shall not recount to those who know them well; filled with a passion for freedom and justice; resolved to build and maintain a society in which these shall be attained by the ordered force of law; trained and disciplined by the persistent, sometimes the desperate, struggle after never-relinquished ideals; feeling in their blood the masterful impulse of the great race that now stands at the top of the world in either hemisphere—of these elements and by this process the Scotch-Irish Bar was in large part formed and moulded, and grew to be the distinguished body it always has been, and is to-day in no less measure than in the past. From its members has come the Scotch-Irish judge, and they and he together should share whatever distinction may belong to his office, or may be added to it by the way he bears himself in so great a place. (Applause.)

(For details of matters treated by Judge McPherson, see Appendix A, page 59, and Appendix B, page 78.)

The President :—

There are here, as our guests, representatives from several kindred associations, whose aim, no less than our own, is the preservation of the memory of the high deeds of a sturdy race, and the perpetuation of that spirit of liberty, truth, and righteousness, which has made our common country great. Extending to them all our cordial greetings of brotherhood, I will now call upon the Rev. Dr. Dana, President of the New England Society, to respond to the toast "Our Sister Societies." (Applause.)

Rev. Stephen W. Dana, D. D. :—

MR. PRESIDENT AND GENTLEMEN OF THE SOCIETY:—This call is most unexpected and is not on the programme. I have been taking my dinner here with real comfort, with no apprehension of anything to follow, and greatly enjoying the speeches that have been given here on this occasion.

But being thus suddenly summoned to my feet, I am very glad to extend to you the hearty greeting of the New England Society, and I think you can give us points. We Yankees think we know something about bragging (laughter), but I don't think "we're in it," as the boys would say. (Laughter.) There are some points, evidently, that are settled that we thought were under discussion. (Laughter.) There has been, as you know, some disagreement among scholars with reference to the members of the human family, whether they all came from one pair or from several, but I am convinced from what I have heard to-night that they all came from one pair, and that Adam and Eve were Scotch-Irish. (Laughter.) Or I am not sure but Adam was Irish and Eve Scotch, and that just after they left Eden they went to Ulster. (Laughter.) But I do rejoice in the vigor and the intelligence and piety of the Scotch-Irish, and I think that the Puritan and the Scotch have always been kindred spirits; they have always contended for similar principles; they have always stood for truth and liberty. I think there has been a feeling, perhaps, on the part of some, that these different societies might awaken a clannish spirit, but I believe that they have, instead, intensified the patriotism of our people. It is a good thing to know "the rock from whence we were hewn." It is a good thing to know what our fathers did, and to consider what the different nationalities have contributed to the life and growth of this great country. There is only one thing about the Scotch-Irish I do not like—they do not know how to speak the English language—I mean to say, in their jokes.

Now, I cannot understand a joke in Scotch dialect. The gentlemen here to-night have all spoken the English language, but many of these Scotch jokes I always have to have interpreted. I am somewhat like Charles Dudley Warner. He was traveling in Germany, in the same compartment with two Englishmen who had been talking together for about half a day, when one of them finally turned to Mr. Warner and said, "Do you speak English?" "No," he said, "I understand English, but I *speak* American." (Laughter.)

Now, I am very glad that the descendants of the Scotch here speak American, and we who are not of the same kin can understand you, while we do have some difficulty in understanding the Scotch dialect. Here let me say that while it is difficult to understand, sometimes, the voice of the Scotchmen, they write most beautiful English. There are no men that are wielding a stronger pen than the Scotch, whether it be in the realm of theology or in the realm of literature; and I wish, as a New Englander, to pay that tribute. New Englanders have done something in the way of literature. We are proud of our orators, our poets, and our scholars, and yet it must be confessed that to-day the Scotch are doing more, perhaps, both for theology and literature, than any other class of men; and I can only say, as a representative of New England, that we are grateful for what your men are doing.

And now, Mr. President, if I should ever have the good fortune to be invited to come here again I shall try to have something in mind to say. I will only, as I sit down, express again my gratification at being present to-night, and rejoice with you that the Scotch-Irish in the past, as well as the Scotch-Irish of to-day, have done and are doing so much for our common country. (Applause.)

The President:—

The famous Dr. Johnson once framed for his dictionary this noted definition of a crab: "A crab is a small red fish, that walks backwards." Concerning this attempt at linguistic exposition a naturalist remarked, that it was quite correct, except that a crab was not necessarily small; that a crab was not generally red; that a crab was not a fish, and did not walk backwards. (Laughter.)

The characterization which the early Scotch-Irish settlers of this State have received at the hands of a certain recent historian bears, at least in the eyes of some of our members, about the same relation to the truth as does Dr. Johnson's famous description. A few exceptions must be made to the general account. If we may accept the criticisms of some of the members of our sister societies, like exceptions must be made out of other accounts in the interesting book of this author.

There is a gentleman with us whom you are all anxious to hear. Having drawn fire from the foe no Scotch-Irishman can refuse the fight, and a fight is not without interest—to us. While he is in the mood for a fray, I would like to submit to Judge Stewart's considerate thought another piece of literature which seems to reflect upon his forebears of the Cumberland Valley. Some time ago I clipped from a publication, which does not circulate widely, a letter written by Dr. Charles Nisbet, in 1790, from his new home in Carlisle to his old home in Scotland. Dr. Nisbet was President of Dickinson College, and a man of much learning. He was not a Scotch-Irishman. He came to America in 1785. Our friend, Sidney George Fisher, has evidently not seen this delightful epistle. I commend it to him for insertion in the revised edition of his book. Here it is from the very hotbed of Pennsylvania Scotch-Irishdom:—

"DEAR SIR:—I was greatly deceived with Regard to the Character of the People of this Country. Had I found them to my liking, I would have endeavoured to engage as many of my old Friends as possible to come over to this Country to make my Banishment here more tolerable to me, but when I found the uncertain Situation of things here, & the fickle and faithless Character of the Inhabitants, my Conscience would not permit me to invite any of my Countrymen hither. (Laughter and applause.) There is nothing in this Country like Scotland except that People here do not walk with their Feet uppermost, but everything else is as contrary as possible. Friendship is at a low Ebb here as well as Religion, only there are more Hypocrites in Friendship than in Religion as the most Part of the People do not even profess to have any. (Much laughter.)

"Yet even in this Country, some are disposed to serve God in the Ministry, & before Six Months there will be Twelve young Men preaching the Gospel who have received their Education at this Seminary. I have endeavoured to introduce the Study of Divinity, which has never been thought of in this country. About Two Years ago, a few young Men here applied to me to give them some Instruction in Divinity.

I have delivered to them already Three hundred & Seventy five Lectures on the first 29 Chapters of the Westminster Confession of Faith, & I hope they will stay with me till I get through it. (Laughter and applause.) I intended likewise to have delivered a few Lectures on the History & Discipline of the Church, on Biblical Criticism & the Pastoral Character, but these I am afraid they will not wait for.

"The Opportunities I have had of serving the Public are indeed few, viz., reading Lectures to a few young Men on the Weekdays & preaching to a thin, lifeless Congregation on Sabbath. But my Sphere of Service may be said to be large in other Respects as our Students are collected from sundry States, & some of them from more than Eight hundred Miles distant.

"The most of our People have as little Patriotism as Religion, & many concurred in the Revolution merely to avoid paying their Debts. I am afraid this Country has not Sense to govern itself. We want men. The public men here are a Set of mean Rogues generally, who mind nothing but Vice & Riot, & please the People that they may live at their Expense, but they have no Knowledge or public Spirit. (Laughter and applause.)

"I regret my leaving Scotland, with Respect to myself, as I live here like the Pelican in the Wilderness, but I submit to it as Dispensation of Providence & endeavor to be serviceable in an obscure Station, though without Friends or Society."

Dr. Nisbet was undoubtedly a man of much learning. (Laughter.) The Scotch-Irish must have sorely vexed his soul. He rests in peace amongst them now in the little cemetery at Carlisle. May he some day arise to know them better. For the rest, I commend him to Judge Stewart, whom I now take great pleasure in presenting to you. (Applause.)

Hon. John Stewart :—

Mr. Chairman:—When I was approached by Mr. Patterson and asked to withdraw my objection to this Society giving you that souvenir, I was generous enough to comply.

Had I known that you proposed to introduce me to this audience by reading Dr. Nisbet's letter, my objection would have stood. I may say, however, in this connection, that that letter is not difficult to explain. It is a genuine letter. The difficulty lies in its interpretation, just as in the case of the recent letter of the Spanish Minister. (Laughter.) It is genuine, but it was not correctly translated. (Laughter.) You have heard already from Dr. Dana that the Scotch is a difficult language to understand. It is still more difficult to translate. If a true translation of that letter were given you would find it to contain no reflection upon the Scotch-Irish of the Cumberland Valley.

Now, I beg to say that I have experienced a very agreeable surprise here to-night. I came expecting censure; not the cordial greeting that you have extended me. I was conscious of the fact that I had offended against Scotch-Irish precept and practice, and had recently engaged in something of a controversy (laughter); and I know nothing is so repugnant to Scotch-Irish feeling as conduct of that kind. (Laughter.) I know that my offense was aggravated by having involved, to some extent, this Scotch-Irish Society in that controversy, since you have been asked to make an apology for including in your published proceedings certain remarks which I made before this Society at its last regular meeting. I found occasion then to refer to a book but recently published in this city, entitled "Pennsylvania—Colony and Commonwealth," and the Society did me the honor to give place to my remarks in its published proceedings. To the criticisms I made, Mr. Sydney George Fisher, the author of the book, has replied in a manner so controversial and personal, and with such persistence in his misrepresentation of fact, as to add to his original offense, and make some further observations necessary. While I should, as a Scotch-Irishman, avoid strife and controversy, I am sure I would offend still more against our faith and practice if, being in the quarrel, I should retire from the contest while my antagonist is in the field.

The exigency thus thrust upon me makes inopportune the speech I had carefully prepared for this occasion. Together last Fall, Dr. Warfield and I made preparation for this evening. He has been able to give you his speech just as he then moulded it—with some little improvement. It is with much regret that circumstances compel me to withhold mine, and substitute for the speech a letter, which with your indulgence I will read as a replication to Mr. Fisher's, in your defense as well as my own.

You have each been furnished with a copy of Mr. Fisher's letter. It is addressed to the Scotch-Irish Society of Pennsylvania, and in it he asks the Society to apologize for including in its published proceedings my remarks, and allowing them "to masquerade as facts of history."

I have adopted his method. I have addressed to him an open letter, a copy of which I sent him this day, and therefore I feel free, if you will indulge me, to read it thus publicly. I do not want you to make the apology he demands until you have had a full presentation of the case. I will detain you but a very few minutes, gentlemen.

CHAMBERSBURG, PA., Feb. 7th, 1898.

Mr. Sydney George Fisher:

SIR:—I beg to acknowledge the receipt of a copy of a printed letter of yours addressed to the members of the Pennsylvania Scotch-Irish Society, under date of February 1st, 1898. Your letter is intended as a reply to some remarks made by me, on the occasion of the last annual banquet of the Society, and which have since been published in their proceedings. The remarks which have called forth this reply were in reference to a work entitled "Pennsylvania—Colony and Commonwealth," of which you are the author. What prompted them was the manifest injustice, as I thought, done you and your book by earlier speakers at the banquet. It is a common complaint among Scotch-Irish people, as you know, that our American historians have not accorded their race the prominence in our early history that it is entitled to; that the Scotch-Irish as a distinct element in our population have been overlooked and ignored. It was in this connection that your book was referred to by several of the speakers, one of whom complained that in the book the Scotch-Irish are scarcely mentioned. (See remarks of Mr. Henry.)

I was fresh from its reading, and knew that not only had you made frequent, but *very* frequent, reference to this race, and had given them a prominence in our early history, which, if it were as honorable as conspicuous, would be just cause for pride in their descendants.

In defending your book against this charge, I used the following language: "On the contrary, sir, it so abounds in them (references to the Scotch-Irish), and all so dishonoring to the race, that in spirit and purpose the book is a studied and deliberate libel."

You do not seem to like the method and manner of my defense. But you must admit that no matter what my motives were, it was the only defense that could be made under the circumstances. That setting it up involved you in a still more serious charge was not my fault. You were entitled to be relieved of the charge of having overlooked and ignored the Scotch-Irish, and I think I made that plain enough. But the whole case had to be presented, and because I did this, you now, in your letter addressed to the members of the Society, put it to "my conscience and Scotch-Irish integrity," to say whether, *in view of certain authorities you cite*, it was proper for me to charge you with studied and deliberate libel, and with being a perverter of the truth of history.

Now, Mr. Fisher, one of us twain has sinned grievously. The offense is mine if I do not sustain the serious charge that I made; it is yours if I do.

In bringing the charge, I was careful to offer specifications with proof. Had you been as careful in your preparation for your history, either your book would not have contained the charges against the Scotch-Irish of which I complain, or there would have been no controversy between us.

My first specification related to the statement contained in your book of the causes which led to the devastation of our western frontier in the years following Braddock's defeat in 1755.

You will agree with me, I am quite sure, when I say that nowhere in all our colonial history was there such widespread devastation wrought as upon our Western frontier during those years; nowhere did savage fury so glut itself with brutal outrage and fiendish massacre. To charge responsibility in any degree upon a civilized people for that horrid tragedy is to hold them up to odium and disgrace. One utters a libel when he publishes that which is defamatory of living or dead; but my charge against you goes beyond this—it includes falsity of statement as well.

I refer now specifically to page 156 of your book. You there say:—

"From 1682 to 1755, a period of seventy-three years, the good faith and honor of the early days when Penn was alive had kept the Indian's tomahawk in his belt. But times had changed; the Scotch-Irish frontiersman, the Walking Purchase, the Albany deed of 1754, and the cunning Frenchmen had done their work, and the scalping knife and hatchet were drawn."

Here is a distinct and unequivocal charge, that the Scotch-Irish frontiersman was in part responsible by his conduct for the awful catastrophe from which his race suffered so extremely. I pass by without comment the dishonorable association you ascribe to the Scotch-Irish frontiersman with the Frenchman, who was the active ally of the savage, and the infamous Walking Purchase, which has always been a synonym for fraud and deceit, and the primacy you give the Scotch-Irish frontiersman in this infamous category, except to remark, that if the element of malice be required to establish the libel, here is abundant evidence from which it might be inferred. Is the statement defamatory? The conduct it charges would be a reproach to even a semi-barbarous people. Is it true? The amazing thing, Mr. Fisher, is that you were willing to write down that charge, in what you intended as an enduring contribution to American history, without a single citation of fact or authority to sustain it. You cite neither author, record, fact, or tradition in support. Is that the way to write impartial history? I charged that the statement was false, and this was my first specification. In your reply you do not even allude to it. It was in connection with this specification that I spoke of the peaceful and amicable relations which had existed between the early settlers of the Kittochtinny Valley and the Indians from

1730 until the Autumn of 1755. In the absence of all citations of authority to support this grievous charge of yours, I had turned to read again the preceding pages to see, if I could, upon what misdoings of this people you had fabricated it. I concluded that you had in mind the alleged unjust occupation of the Indian's land without treaty or purchase, and hence my reference to the actual situation here at the period referred to. If I at all understand your reply, you disavow this, and yet on page 126 of your book I find this:—

"The Scotch-Irish and Germans west of the Susquehanna had been entering on Indian land which had not yet been purchased by the proprietors. This was now a common offense and the people had become accustomed to the Indian complaints of it."

In your reply you distinctly say that you never made any such assertion, that is, that there was any improper appropriation of land by the settlers east of the Kittochtinny. This whole valley lies west of the Susquehanna and east of the Kittochtinny, and at the period of which you write it was the most populous region on the frontier.

Speaking to this point you say that if I had confined myself to the land east of the Kittochtinny range, instead of east of the Tuscarora, you might have said that you knew of none that had been improperly appropriated. The obvious reply to this is, that had you confined yourself to the land west of the Kittochtinny range, there would have been little occasion for reference to it on my part, seeing how insignificant the encroachments beyond that range were. You distinctly charge that the settlers "west of the Susquehanna" had been making these encroachments. If your reference was to those west of the Kittochtinny, why did you not say so? Why include all this valley region lying between the river and the mountain, in which was to be found the only considerable settlement west of the river? Your inexactness of expression, if your meaning was what you say it was, would hardly have been more marked had you said west of Philadelphia.

The above extract, notwithstanding your denial, which latter is in direct contradiction of the text of your book, I submit fully warranted me in concluding that it was this alleged trespass upon Indian land you had in mind when you made the charge referred to; especially so when considered in connection with this additional extract taken from page 113:—

"To the ordinary Scotch-Irish or German frontiersman, the buying of land from the Indians seemed like a farce. That good, rich land which would support a family of white people and Christians should not be cleared and cultivated because a band of roving, drunken, and dirty savages claimed it, seemed supremely ridiculous. The frontiersman would not accept such a motion seriously, or believe that any one would seriously enforce it. He went out on the land believing that the Government would be sensible and allow him to remain."

I cite these references from your book, merely to show what reason you give your readers to conclude that it is upon this data you base your charge. If we are now to understand that this is a wrong conclusion, then, so far as your book discloses, the charge that the scalping knife and hatchet were drawn in consequence of Scotch-Irish conduct rests upon nothing whatever.

You avoid the issue, Mr. Fisher, when in your reply you undertake to show that there was unlawful appropriation of land west of the Kittochtinny. What has that to do with the subject of our present controversy? If it were at all important, I would gladly undertake to instruct you upon this matter, and show you how these western encroachments were not only insignificant in themselves, but that they were never associated in the savage mind with the incursions that followed Braddock's defeat, and did not in the least contribute to them. If you desire to pursue that inquiry, let me commend to your careful study a little book which you will find upon the shelves of the Historical Society of Pennsylvania, entitled, "A Tribute to the Principles, Virtues, &c., of the Irish and Scotch Early Settlers of Pennsylvania," written by a very distinguished citizen of this valley, long since dead, but whose fame survives, the Hon. George Chambers.

I pass to the second specification in the charge against you of libel. It was, that out of the incident of the killing of the Indians at Lancaster by the Paxtang boys, you "fabricated the accusation that it was the Scotch-Irish who introduced lynch law into this country."

I quote from page 236 of your book:—

"This was probably the first instance of the administration of the lynch law, as it is called, which has now become so common among us that hundreds of lynchings take place in the United States every year; and so far as it is a benefit, the Scotch-Irish may be given the credit for its introduction."

In your reply you make no allusion to this specification. You are as silent with respect to it as the first; and yet these two matters I specified in my address, and upon these I rested chiefly the charge. You seem to think that it is a sufficient answer to convict me of historical inaccuracy with respect to some collateral matter, forgetting that it is your reliability and reputation as a historian that is in issue, not mine. Is it any answer to the charge I bring to say that James Wilson and Provost Smith were Scotchmen, and not Scotch-Irishmen? a distinction you make in your reply, but which, as you will see by referring to page 394, you do not observe in your book. Your appeal is to my conscience and Scotch-Irish integrity, with respect to this charge of libel, "in view of the authorities you cite." Need I ask you, do you cite any authority either in your book or in your reply touching these broad and defamatory statements which I have cited from your book?

Who but you, Mr. Fisher, ever said that the Scotch-Irish are entitled to the credit of having introduced lynch law into this country, and that to their example and influence is to be traced the barbarous practices which disgrace us as a people in this regard to-day? I know it has long been a mooted question as to the origin of lynch law; that many different notions prevail in regard to it; I know also that the Lancaster incident has been variously commented upon and discussed by eminent historians and others, and I feel quite sure that the historic connection between the two never occurred to any one but yourself. I enter no defense for the Paxtang boys; but I have a right to demand your authority for saying that the killing of the Conestoga Indians was the first application of lynch law that occurred in this country, admitting that it was lynch law. I do not care to stop to distinguish between that killing and lynch law; the distinction will readily enough occur to any one familiar with the incident and at all dispassionate, but I again challenge you for authority for your statement.

Again, admitting it to have been the application of lynch law, what reason is there in your deduction that the credit for it is to be given to the Scotch-Irish? You assert that those engaged in the killing were Scotch-Irish frontiersmen. On page 235, you speak of them as having been "under the preaching of the famous John Elder, who had often addressed an armed congregation with his own rifle resting beside him in the pulpit;" and you say that fifty-seven of these men, that is, as you would clearly have your reader understand, it was fifty-seven of these typical, representative church-going Scotch-Irish Presbyterians, who killed the Conestoga Indians. Listen to what the same Rev. John Elder, a Scotch-Irish Presbyterian pastor, says in his letter to Governor Penn, dated 16th December, 1763, with reference to this matter:—

"I thought it my duty to give you this early notice, that an action of this nature may not be imputed to these frontier settlements. For I know not one person of judgment or prudence that has been in anywise concerned in it; but it has been done by some hot-headed, ill-advised persons, and especially by such I imagine as suffered much in their relations by the ravages committed by the late Indian war."

I pass now to the third specification, the second as it appears in my remarks, but which for reasons you will understand I make the third. It is the only one you refer to.

I attributed to you an antipathy to the Scotch-Irish, and in this way accounted for the unfairness of your narration. Simply to illustrate, and for no other purpose, I referred to your statements in regard to the conduct of the Scotch-Irish in connection with Bouquet's expedition. You treat it as though it were the chief, if not only, thing upon which the charges I made depend. The language I used was this: "With equal recklessness of statement, and in like spirit of unfairness, he charges that in 1763, when Bouquet passed the Valley on his way to the Ohio, and beyond, to suppress the conspiracy of Pontiac, this people were too indifferent or cowardly to recruit his ranks and too mean to supply him transportation."

In your reply you quote from page 225 of your book as follows:—

"Not a man of the Scotch-Irish frontiersmen joined him. They were slow at furnishing him with wagons and caused him many delays. They were indeed broken and demoralized, and stayed at home, they said, to protect their families, and moreover they believed that the colonel and his sick list were doomed."

In your attempted vindication you say:—

"In the above passage I charge no one with cowardice. I do not say that they were too mean to furnish transportation; I say that they were slow about it, and I give reasons for all their conduct which would satisfy any one in a reasonable frame of mind."

You are quite correct, Mr. Fisher, so far as regards the letter of your text. But I presume you are familiar with the office of the innuendo in pleading. It is not necessary that the libel be apparent in the letters and words used. The innuendo supplies the meaning and spirit.

Will you be good enough to tell me why you regarded the fact that no Scotch-Irish frontiersman joined Bouquet, of sufficient importance historically to find a place in your book? Is it not equally true that no English or German or Scotch (for you distinguish between the Scotch and Scotch-Irish) or Quaker joined him? Do you say that you were silent as to them because, at Carlisle, Bouquet was in the heart of a Scotch-Irish settlement? But Carlisle was simply a point on the long march, and to reach that place Bouquet had to march through a still more populous district, wherein dwelt all these different races and people; and even when at Carlisle any appeal which he might have made must have reached these other districts, for they were by no means remote. Was Bouquet's expedition intended merely for the deliverance of the Scotch-Irish on the frontier? Did not all the people of the Province have like stake in it, and did not equal obligation rest upon all in the emergency?

The fact is, and I repeat it, Bouquet did not call for additional soldiers in the sense you would have your readers understand. He was a British officer, in command of British troops. He was about to attempt a long march through an unbroken wilderness. Having in mind the fate of Braddock and the stealthiness of Indian warfare, he sought to engage a body of frontiersmen, to serve not as enlisted soldiers, but as an irregular force to act as flankers on the march. His need for such men would only become great after reaching Fort Bedford. He expected to engage them at Carlisle, but the condition of things there—and we shall see presently what that was—made it impracticable; and he used his Highlanders for the purpose until Bedford was reached, and he there obtained the requisite number of frontiersmen. Parkman in his "Conspiracy of Pontiac," vol. 2, page 58, gives the number as thirty. You say you "will leave the Judge and Parkman to fight it out between them." No candid reader, Mr. Fisher, will for a moment suppose that there is any disagreement of fact between Parkman and me; what you call a fight is between Mr. Parkman and yourself. You seek to give to his narrative a meaning which his text will not warrant, and which he never could have intended.

In your book and your reply, you evidently intend to convey the idea that Bouquet required a larger force than he had, and invited volunteers to his ranks. On page 232, again recurring to the subject, without any apparent purpose other than to expose this people to obloquy, you say, speaking of the Scotch-Irish:—

"Their loud complaints against the Quakers and the Assembly, and their demands for protection and vengeance, may seem somewhat inconsistent when we remember that they declined to follow Bouquet on his expedition to save Fort Pitt, although that was evidently the only plan that would permanently check invasion and secure the protection and vengeance they desired."

It resolves itself into this: because Bouquet found it impracticable to engage at Carlisle a body of thirty trained and active frontiersmen, accustomed to the ways and methods of the savage, and familiar with the country he was about to march into, you as a historian feel justified in making the statement that the Scotch-Irish "declined to follow Bouquet in his expedition," and in recording it as a fact entitled to a permanent place in our colonial history, that "not a man of the Scotch-Irish frontiersmen joined him." And this, too, in spite of the fact that when he reached Bedford, where he had actual need of this peculiar service, he got all that he wanted from this very race of people.

You say you charged no one with cowardice. My language was that you charged that "this people were too indifferent or cowardly to recruit his (Bouquet's) ranks." There is no escape, Mr. Fisher, from the conclusion that you mention the circumstance referred to as a reflection upon the Scotch-Irish. If they came short of their duty—and that they did, you certainly charge—it must have been through cowardice or indifference.

On page 237 you say, "These wild Scotch-Irish, it was said, had been crying aloud for protection, and yet were afraid to assist in protecting themselves by marching with Bouquet to save Fort Pitt." *You* do not say that they were *afraid*, but you introduce here a charge of cowardice in this connection, for which no one can be held accountable, and allow it to stand in explanation of the conduct you have described. In the face of this extract from your book, you say in your reply that no one but myself ever suggested that they were cowards.

You say that you "give reasons for their conduct which would satisfy any one in a reasonable frame of mind."

Excuse me, Mr. Fisher, if I feel compelled to discredit somewhat your candor in this statement. The reasons you state are these: "They were indeed broken and demoralized, and stayed at home, they said, to protect their families." The reason *you* give is that they were broken and demoralized; the reason *they* gave was that they were needed to protect their families. You are willing to take upon yourself as a historian the responsibility for the first statement; but you leave the reader to give what credence he chooses to the reason which these people themselves gave.

In order to see how unfairly you have used this incident against this people, and that your prejudice against them may fully appear, it is necessary to understand clearly what the actual situation at Carlisle was at the period referred to. We will not learn this from your book. Let us get something authentic. I know you have but a poor opinion of Parkman (your estimate of him will be found on page 179 of your book), but I will venture to quote him, for by every one but yourself he will be accepted as both intelligent and veracious. I cite from "Conspiracy of Pontiac," vol. 2, page 44:—

"The scenes which daily met his (Bouquet's) eye might well have moved him to pity as well as indignation. When he reached Carlisle, at the end of June, he found every building in the fort, every house, barn, and hovel in the little town, crowded with the families of settlers, driven from their homes by the terror of the tomahawk. Wives made widows, children made orphans, wailed and moaned in anguish and despair. On the 13th of July he wrote to Amherst: 'The list of the people known to be killed increases very fast every hour. The desolation of so many families, reduced to the last extremity of want and misery; the despair of those who have lost their parents, relations, and friends, with the cries of distracted women and children who fill the streets, form a scene painful to humanity, and impossible to describe.'"

Since compelled to go outside your book to find this description of the most painful and tragic incident in our colonial history, and have recourse to Parkman, I must be allowed to give in excuse for so doing an extract from your reply. You there say:—

"The reason that the New Englanders have been able to write the history of the country, and that others have not, is because that, while taking care of their own point of view, they have written on the whole with remarkable accuracy, while the others have usually produced miserable trash for which no one has any respect and which few care to read."

Keeping in view the picture which Parkman and Bouquet present of the distressing and deplorable condition of these Scotch-Irish, but which is so inadequately and feebly represented in your book that it would scarcely excite the attention of the average reader, and keeping in mind also what Bouquet's actual demands were, I ask you in all candor, Mr. Fisher, what is the significance of your repeated statement that "not a man of the Scotch-Irish frontiersmen joined him"? What is the significance of your unwillingness to recognize the imperative necessity that was upon this people, of looking after and protecting their families in this dire extremity? Why could you not state it as a fact? Why must you qualify it by saying that *"they* said" it?

I have thus briefly considered the matters contained in your book, upon which I rested the charge that the book was a studied and deliberate libel on the Scotch-Irish of the colony. I am willing to leave it to the impartial mind to say whether, in making the charge, I was either extravagant or unjudicial.

I now pass to some collateral matters which you discuss in your reply, with no other purpose that I can discover than to avert attention from the only issue that was between us.

In the course of my remarks I stated that while you regarded the circumstance that no Scotch-Irish frontiersman joined Bouquet an important historical fact, you thought it a fact too insignificant for mention that "in the previous campaign this same people sent twenty-five hundred of its chosen men, under the lead of John Armstrong, to march in the van of Forbes' army to the Ohio."

You will at once observe the difference between the statement as I have above given it, and the published report of my remarks. It is the difference of a word. What I meant to say, and what I think I did say, was that this people—meaning the Scotch-Irish—and not the Kittochtinny settlement, had sent twenty-five hundred of their chosen men into the service. I meant to speak of the Pennsylvania provincial force under Armstrong as a Scotch-Irish army, and wanted to be so understood. I am now discussing a matter wholly aside from the subject of our original controversy; for again I beg to remind you that the question at issue between us is whether you libelled a race of people and are a perverter of the truth of history; and that it can have no bearing whatever upon that issue to show that I was incorrect in some collateral statement. You have devoted two pages and more of your letter to a wholly irrelevant matter, and have succeeded in convicting me of error. I frankly admit it. I had in mind the entire provincial force and I stated it at twenty-five hundred. You say it was twenty-seven hundred, and I find on further examination that you are correct in your figures. Did I exceed just limits in an address on such an occasion as was this—remember I was not writing history—in claiming that Armstrong's force was a Scotch-Irish army? The Scotch-

Irish were the fighting stock and capital of the colony. I cannot establish from the muster rolls that this army was made up exclusively of Scotch-Irish, nor is it necessary that I should. Knowing the peculiarities of the several elements of our population at that time, and their respective numbers, it is an easy, and I think quite safe, inference that in that army the Scotch-Irish largely predominated. We had the Quaker, the German, and the Scotch-Irish, we had other elements, too, but comparatively insignificant in numbers. The Quakers did not contribute at all; a very large proportion of the German population held to like peace principles with the Quaker, and were non-combatants. Where was the fighting force to come from but the Scotch-Irish? It is true, Mr. Fisher, that at the close of the Revolutionary war it was said by those who knew, and the statement has never been contradicted, that in this valley, where these Scotch-Irish were to be found in greatest numbers, there was scarcely an able-bodied man who had not at some period of the war been engaged in service. Was I extravagant in claiming, with such a record as this at a period only a little later, Armstrong's as a Scotch-Irish army, because it was not exclusively so? You say you have examined the muster rolls of some of the companies, and you find that some of the soldiers were even from other States. Does this circumstance make that army any less distinctively a Pennsylvania army?

I am sorry indeed that a mistake in the types or an inadvertence of mine, which substituted for the word people the word settlement, should have exposed you to the laughter and ridicule of the gentlemen of the Historical Society of Pennsylvania, by prompting you to inquire of them whether it was true in fact that a settlement of eight thousand people had given twenty-five hundred of their "chosen men" to Forbes' army. I am not sure that you have not exposed yourself to still greater ridicule by devoting more than two pages of your letter to disproving it as a fact.

Another side issue you raise. You say:—

"By the way, what does he mean by saying that his twenty-five hundred marched in the van of Forbes' army? Besides the Pennsylvania troops, that army of about seven thousand men was composed of British regulars, Virginia troops, Maryland troops, and North Carolina troops. If the Judge has any information about the order of march in that scramble through the woods and mountains which Parkman so vividly describes, his Scotch-Irish generosity should furnish us with it, for it would be extremely interesting."

I will accommodate you, Mr. Fisher; but does it not occur to you that it ought to be somewhat humiliating for one who asks to be accredited as a historian of his State to apply to one no better informed than you think me, for information which is to be found in Bancroft's History of the United States? Have you ever heard of the book?

On page 206, vol. 3, Bancroft says:—

"Every encampment was so planned as to hasten the issue. On the 13th the veteran Armstrong, who had proved his superior skill in leading troops rapidly and secretly through the wilderness, pushed forward with one thousand men, and in five days threw up defenses within seventeen miles of Fort Duquesne. On the 15th Washington, who followed, was on Chestnut Ridge; on the 17th at Bushy Run. * * * On Saturday, the 25th of November, the little army moved on in a body; and at evening the youthful hero (Washington) could point out *to Armstrong and the hardy provincials, who marched in front,* to the Highlanders and royal Americans, to Forbes himself, the meeting of the rivers."

A single word now as to the high regard you profess in your reply for these Scotch-Irish. You say you admire them "when they behave themselves, especially the old type, who were usually right with their facts," and that you believe most people admire them.

You protest too much, Mr. Fisher. You have recorded your estimate of these Scotch-Irish "of the old type" on page 124 of your book, and it is worth repeating in this connection. You there say:—

"The reason for this feeling of the Indian (his respect for and confidence in the Quaker) was not merely the recollection of fair treatment from Penn, but a certain consistency he had observed in Penn's followers. A savage is very quick to detect hypocrisy or a difference between preaching and practice; and when he heard Catholic or Presbyterian missionaries talk of gentleness, honesty, forgiveness, and sobriety, and looked about him at the Catholic or *Presbyterian frontiersmen* and traders who habitually cheated him, and whom he had often seen swearing, drunk, and murdering, there was no use in telling him that they were the exceptions, and not living up to the faith that was true in spite of them."

You have a queer way of showing your appreciation and admiration of these Scotch-Irish "of the old type," Mr. Fisher. I quote again from page 239:—

> "As in the previous war, there had been a violent outburst of party feeling, so now there was another. The Scotch-Irish were soon in the full flame of another insurrection, not unlike the Whiskey Rebellion, in which they indulged themselves almost thirty years afterward."

You introduce the Whiskey Rebellion into your narrative of the colony to emphasize, I suppose, your admiration for the race. No other purpose is apparent. In the next edition of your book would it not be well for you to explain just what you mean by saying that this insurrection, as you call it, was not unlike the Whiskey Rebellion? It is a little obscure to the ordinary mind.

Again recurring to the Conestoga Indian incident—without any apparent purpose, except to emphasize your admiration—on page 251 you say:—

> "The relief experienced after Bouquet's victory at Bushy Run, or after [the Scotch-Irish victory in the jail at Lancaster, as some insisted, was only a lull."

On page 288 you speak of them as having been nourished on revolutions, and of the keenness of their appetite for such diet. On page 232 you speak of their not being much interested in invasions of the enemy's country, "and *apparently* because they thought it more important to stay at home and protect their families, while the regular troops attended to the distant expeditions."

On page 162 you characterize them as an uncouth people.

In spite of these statements and characterizations in your book—and I forbear citing others only because I am tired— you protest that, in common with most people, you admire the Scotch-Irish "of the old type." It may be that you do, but the reader of your book, allow me to say, will search its pages in vain to discover on what this admiration rests. The only inference that can be drawn from the manifest disagreement between the opinion expressed in your book, and that expressed in your reply to me, is, that the admiration you now profess has come with the fuller knowledge and better understanding of Scotch-Irish history and character you have derived from reading the published proceedings of the Society. If my remarks which appear therein have in any degree contributed to your enlightenment and conversion, I am more than compensated.

The injustice you have done that virile race of German settlers, who did so much to give character and stability to the institutions and civilization of our colonial period, is quite as marked as your unfair treatment of the Scotch-Irish. I can only hope that some descendant of this race will yet so instruct you that your appreciation and admiration of the German frontiersman will be proportionately increased. I would cheerfully undertake this task myself, but for the fact that I am quite certain that other and abler defenders of the colonial German will not be wanting. To them and their tender mercies I commend you and your book.

In conclusion, you will excuse me, Mr. Fisher, if I pass unnoticed your uncomplimentary allusions to myself. I have already devoted too much space to collateral matters. When I sat down, it was to answer your appeal to my "conscience and Scotch-Irish integrity" to say whether I had unjustly charged you with a libel. To make answer, I had to review the charge and the matters to which it related. This I have tried to do, and I have sought to do it in such a way that even you must see that I would be false to history and the people from whom I have my descent if I were to retract or even modify the charge in any respect.

The only atonement you can make for the serious offense you have committed is to confess it. I am not without hope that repentance and a better mind may yet come to you.

Your obedient servant,

JOHN STEWART.

(Great applause.)

(For letter from Sydney George Fisher, to which the above is a reply, see Appendix C, page 107.)

Now, Mr. Chairman, I want to say that I have tried to treat Mr. Fisher courteously; I know I have treated him fairly.

If, in the judgment of this Society, an apology is necessary, I shall not resist it, and if in your judgment you shall conclude that I am a proper subject for discipline, I am ready to receive it. (Applause.)

The President:—

This Society, at least, has never entertained the fear that a Scotch-Irishman would run away before he had fought to a finish. Judge Stewart stands acquitted before us.

There is an act of graceful remembrance that would become us to-night. Ex-Chief Justice Agnew is now in his eighty-ninth year. He cannot be with us. I would suggest that the greetings of this assembly be conveyed to him.

It was thereupon, on motion—

Resolved, That the greetings of this assembly be conveyed to ex-Chief Justice Agnew.

The President:—

Thanking you, gentlemen, for the great kindness you have shown to me on this occasion, and expressing to you again my high appreciation of the honor you have bestowed upon me, I have now the very great pleasure of presenting to you my successor in this office, Justice Henry W. Williams, of the Supreme Court of Pennsylvania. (Applause.)

Justice Henry W. Williams: —

GENTLEMEN OF THE SCOTCH-IRISH SOCIETY:—I would be unwilling to accept the duties of the position to which you have so kindly called me without first expressing my heartfelt gratitude for the honor which the selection involves. I trust that I shall be able to keep within the line of safe precedents and follow the footsteps of my illustrious predecessors in the discharge of the very simple duties that devolve upon me as your presiding officer. Of one thing I feel sure, that my term of office will impose upon me the exercise of no arbitrary power, and no administrative burdens; for a society of Scotch-

Irishmen have a settled habit, and have had for hundreds of years, of governing themselves or knowing the reason why. My duties will therefore be light and agreeable, and will amount to little more than looking on while the Society governs itself in an orderly and dignified manner. The hour for speech making to-night has already passed, and has been profitably and pleasantly filled. I will content myself therefore by repeating once more the assurance that I thank you sincerely for the honor you have done me and expressing the hope that I may wear it worthily.

The banquet was then adjourned.

APPENDIX A.

PROVINCIAL JUDGES.
CHIEF JUSTICES OF THE SUPREME COURT.
Arthur Cook . . . . 1680–1684.
Nicholas Moore . . . . 1684–1685.
James Harrison (declined) 1685–
Arthur Cook . . . . 1686–1690.
John Simcock . . . . 1690–1693.
Andrew Robson . . . . 1693–1699.
Edward Shippen . . . . 1699–1701.
John Guest . . . . August 20, 1701–April 10, 1703.
William Clark . . . . April 10, 1703–1705.
John Guest . . . . 1705–1706.
Roger Mompesson . . . . April 17, 1706–1715.
Joseph Growden, Jr. . . . . 1715–1718.
David Lloyd . . . . 1718–1731.
Isaac Norris (declined) . . . . April 9, 1731–
James Logan . . . . August 20, 1731–1739.
Jeremiah Langhorne . . . . August 13, 1739–1743.
John Kinsey . . . . April 5, 1743–
William Allen (vice Kinsey, deceased), September 20, 1750–
Benjamin Chew . . . . April 29, 1774–1776.

PUISNE JUDGES.
William Welch (died July, 1684) . . May 29, 1684–July, 1684.
William Wood . . . . May 29, 1684–July 14, 1685.
Robert Turner . . . . May 29, 1684–1685.
John Eckley . . . . May 29, 1684–1686.
William Clark (vice Welch) . . . . 1684–1693.
John Claypoole . . . . 1685–1686.
Arthur Cook . . . . 1685–1686.
John Simcock . . . . 1686–1690.
John Cann . . . . 1686–1690.
James Harrison . . . . 1686–1690.
Joseph Growden . . . . 1690–1693.
Peter Alricks . . . . September 5, 1690–1693.
Thomas Wynn . . . . September 5, 1690–1693.
Griffith Jones . . . . 1690–1693.
Edward Blake . . . . 1690–1698.
William Salway . . . . 1693–1698.
John Cann . . . . 1693–August 10, 1694.
Edward Blake . . . . 1693–1698.

Anthony Morris (vice Cann) . . . . . . August 10, 1694–1698.
Joseph Growden . . . . 1698–1699.
Cornelius Empson . . . . 1698–1701.
William Biles . . . . 1699–1701.
John Guest . . . . 1699–1701.
Joseph Growden (declined) 1701–
Caleb Pusey (declined) 1701–
Thomas Masters . . . . 1701–1705.
William Clark . . . . 1702–1703.
Capt. Samuel Tinney . . . . 1702–1711.
John Guest . . . . 1703–1705.
Edward Shippen . . . . 1703–1705.
Jasper Yeates . . . . 1705–1711.
William Trent . . . . 1705–1715.
Joseph Growden, Jr. . . . . 1705–1715.
George Roche (resigned) . . . . 1711–1715.
Anthony Palmer . . . . 1711–1715.
William Trent . . . . 1715–1722.
Jonathan Dickinson . . . . 1715–1718.
Robert Asheton . . . . 1715–1718.
Richard Hill . . . . 1718–1731.
Robert Asheton . . . . 1722–1726.
William Trent . . . . 1724–(?)
Jeremiah Langhorne . . . . 1726–1739.
John French . . . . July 25, 1726–
Dr. Thomas Graeme . . . . 1731–1750.
Thomas Griffitts . . . . 1739–1743.
William Till . . . . 1743–1750.
Lawrence Growden . . . . 1750–1764.
Caleb Cowpland (died 1758) . . . . 1750–1758.
William Coleman (vice Cowpland) . . . . . 1758–1764.
Alexander Stedman . . . . 1764–1767.
John Lawrence . . . . 1767–1776.
Thomas Willing . . . . 1767–1776.
John Morton . . . . 1774–1776.

COURT OF CHANCERY.
CHANCELLORS.

Sir William Keith.   Patrick Gordon.   George Thomas.

COURT OF VICE ADMIRALTY.
JUDGES.

William Markham . . . . 1693.
Robert Quarry . . . . 1695.
Roger Mompesson . . . . 1703.
William Assheton . . . . 1718.
Josiah Rolfe . . . . June 25, 1724.

Joseph Brown . . . . March 18, 1724–1725.
Charles Read . . . . April 21, 1735.
Andrew Hamilton . . . . September 11, 1737.
Thomas Hopkinson . . . . January 17, 1744–1745.
Patrick Baird . . . . December 12, 1749.
Edward Shippen, Jr. . . . . November 22, 1752–1761.
George Ross . . . . 1776.

DEPUTY JUDGE.
Isaac Miranda . . . . July 19, 1727.

JUSTICES OF OYER AND TERMINER AND GAOL DELIVERY FOR PHILADELPHIA, BUCKS, AND CHESTER.

Andrew Hamilton . . . . October 26, 1730–1732.
William Allen . . . . October 26, 1730.
Thomas Graeme . . . . April 28, 1732.

JUDGES OF THE COMMONWEALTH.

(Italics denote Scottish or Scotch-Irish descent; a star, absence of either strain; roman type without a star, that no information has been obtained.)

CHIEF JUSTICES OF THE SUPREME COURT.

Joseph Reed (declined) . . . . March 20, 1777.
Thomas McKean . . . . July 28, 1777.
*Edward Shippen.   *John Meredith Read.
*,William Tilghman.   *Daniel Agnew.*
John Bannister Gibson.   *George Sharswood.
Jeremiah S. Black.   *Ulysses Mercur.
Ellis Lewis. (Scottish.)   *Isaac G. Gordon.*
Walter H. Lowrie.   *Edward M. Paxson.
*George W. Woodward.   *James P. Sterrett.*
James Thompson.

ASSOCIATE JUSTICES OF THE SUPREME COURT.

*William Augustus Atlee . . . . April 2, 1777.
*John Evans . . . . August 16, 1777.
George Bryan . . . . April 5, 1780.
*Jacob Rush . . . . February 26, 1784.
*Jasper Yeates.   *Frederick Smith.*
*William Bradford.   *John Ross.*
Thomas Smith.   *John Kennedy.*
H. H. Brackenridge. (Scottish.)   *Thomas Sergeant.
Thomas Duncan. (Scottish.)   *Thomas Burnside.* (Scottish.)
Molton Cropper Rodgers.   *Richard Coulter.*
Charles Huston.   *Thomas S. Bell.*
John Tod. (Scottish.)   *George Chambers.*

John C. Knox.
James Armstrong.
William Strong.
William A. Porter.
*Gaylord Church.
*H. W. Williams. (Allegheny.)
*Warren J. Woodward.
*John Trunkey.
*Henry Green.

Silas M. Clark.
Henry W. Williams. (Tioga.)
*Alfred Hand.
J. B. McCollum.
*James T. Mitchell.
*Christopher Heydrick.
John Dean.
Samuel G. Thompson.
*D. Newlin Fell.

COURT OF ADMIRALTY OF THE STATE.

George Ross . . . . March 1, 1779.
*Francis Hopkinson . . . . July 16, 1779.

HIGH COURT OF ERRORS AND APPEALS.
(Under Act of February 28, 1780.)

Joseph Reed . . . . November 20, 1780.
Thomas McKean . . . . November 20, 1780.
*William A. Atlee . . . . November 20, 1780.
*John Evans . . . . November 20, 1780.
George Bryan . . . . November 20, 1780.
James Smith . . . . November 20, 1780.
*Henry Wynkoop . . . . November 20, 1780.
*Francis Hopkinson . . . . November 20, 1780.
William Moore . . . . November 14, 1781.
*John Dickinson . . . . November 7, 1782.
*James Bayard . . . . March 18, 1783.
Samuel Miles . . . . April 7, 1783.
*Jacob Rush . . . . February 26, 1784.
*Edward Shippen . . . . September 16, 1784.
*Benjamin Franklin . . . . October 18, 1785.
*Thomas Mifflin . . . . November 5, 1788.

(As Reorganized under Act of April 13, 1791.)

*Benjamin Chew . . . . September 30, 1791.
Thomas McKean . . . . April 17, 1791.
*Edward Shippen . . . . April 17, 1791.
*Jasper Yeates . . . . April 17, 1791.
*William Bradford . . . . August 20, 1791.
*James Biddle . . . . September 1, 1791.
*William A. Atlee . . . . September 1, 1791.
*Jacob Rush . . . . September 1, 1791.
James Riddle . . . . September 1, 1791.
Alexander Addison (Scottish) . . . . . September 1, 1791.
John Joseph Henry . . . . November, 1793.
Thomas Smith . . . . January 31, 1794.
John D. Coxe . . . . April 6, 1797.
Hugh H. Brackenridge (Scottish) . . . . December 18, 1799.
*William Tilghman . . . . July 31, 1805.

SUPERIOR COURT.

*Charles E. Rice (President).
*Edward N. Willard.
John J. Wickham.
*James A. Beaver.
*Howard J. Reeder.
George B. Orlady.
*Peter P. Smith.
William W. Porter.

ADAMS COUNTY.

John Joseph Henry . . . . December 16, 1793.
*Walter Franklin . . . . January 18, 1811.
*Daniel Durkee . . . . May 4, 1835.
William N. Irvine . . . . February 6, 1846.
*R. J. Fisher.   William McClean.
David Wills.   S. McC. Swope.

ALLEGHENY COUNTY.

Alexander Addison (Scottish) . . . . August 1, 1791.
Samuel Roberts . . . . April 30, 1803.
William Wilkins . . . . December 18, 1820.
*Charles Shaler . . . . June 5, 1824.
Robert C. Grier . . . . May 2, 1833.
Trevanian B. Dallas (Scottish) . . . . May 5, 1835.
Benjamin Patton, Jr. . . . . July 1, 1839.
Hopewell Hepburn . . . . September 17, 1844.
Walter H. Lowrie . . . . August 20, 1846.
William B. McClure . . . . January 31, 1850.
Walter Forward . . . . November 7, 1851.
Peter C. Shannon . . . . November 27, 1852.
*John W. Maynard . . . . April 16, 1859.
Thomas Mellon . . . . November 8, 1859.
James P. Sterrrett . . . . January 4, 1862.
David Ritchie . . . . May 22, 1862.
Edwin H. Stowe . . . . November 4, 1862.
*Frederick H. Collier.   J. W. Over.
*Moses Hampton.   Christopher Magee.
*H. W. Williams.   J. F. Slagle.
J. M. Kirkpatrick.   J. M. Kennedy.
J. W. F. White.   W. D. Porter.
Thomas Ewing.   S. A. McClung.
John H. Bailey.   R. S. Frazer.
*C. S. Fetterman.   John D. Shafer.
W. G. Hawkins.

ARMSTRONG COUNTY.

John Young . . . . March 1, 1806.
Thomas White . . . . December 13, 1806.
Jeremiah N. Burrell . . . . March 25, 1847.
John C. Knox . . . . April 11, 1848.
*Joseph Buffington . . . . November 5, 1855.
J. A. Logan.   J. B. Neale.
Jackson Boggs.   Calvin Rayburn.

BEAVER COUNTY.

Samuel Roberts . . . . April 30, 1803.
William Wilkins . . . . December 18, 1820.
John Bredin . . . . April 18, 1831.
Lawrence McGuffin.   John J. Wickham.
*Henry Hice.   J. S. Wilson.

BEDFORD COUNTY.

Bernard Dougherty.
George Woods.
James Riddle . . . . February 24, 1794.
Jonathan Walker . . . . March 1, 1806.
Charles Huston . . . . July 1, 1818.
John Tod (Scottish) . . . . June 8, 1824.
Alexander Thompson . . . . June 25, 1827.
Jeremiah S. Black . . . . March 30, 1842.
F. M. Kimmel . . . . November 6, 1851.
James Nill . . . . November 20, 1861.
Alexander King.   *W. J. Baer.
D. W. Rowe.   *J. H. Longenecker.
William Maclay Hall.

BERKS COUNTY.

*Jacob Rush . . . . August 17, 1793.
*John Spayd.
Robert Porter . . . . July 6, 1809.
*Garrick Mallory . . . . April 1, 1831.
John Banks . . . . April 1, 1836.
*J. P. Jones . . . . March 13, 1847.
David F. Gordon . . . . April 6, 1849.
*W. J. Woodward . . . . November 21, 1861.
*J. Hagenman.   *J. N. Ermentrout.
*H. Van Reed.   *G. A. Endlich.
*A. H. Sassaman.   *H. W. Bland.
*H. H. Swartz.

BLAIR COUNTY.

Jeremiah S. Black.
George Taylor . . . . April 6, 1849.
John Dean.
*A. L. Landis.
Martin Bell.

BRADFORD COUNTY.

John B. Gibson.
Thomas Burnside.
*Edward Herrick . . . . July 7, 1818.
John N. Conyngham (Scottish) . . . . March 25, 1839.
*Horace Williston . . . . April 6, 1849.
*David Wilmot . . . . November 6, 1851.
*Darius Bullock . . . . August 8, 1857.
*Ulysses Mercur . . . . March 19, 1861.
*Ferris B. Streater . . . . March 4, 1865.
*P. D. Morrow.
*B. M. Peck.

BUCKS COUNTY.
*James Biddle.
John D. Coxe . . . . June 19, 1797.
Bird Wilson (Scottish) . . . . March 1, 1806.
John Ross . . . . January 13, 1818.
*John Fox . . . . April 16, 1830.
Thomas Burnside (Scottish) . . . . March 30, 1841.
*David Krause . . . . January 31, 1845.
*Daniel M. Smyser . . . . November 6, 1851.
*Henry Chapman . . . . November 20, 1851.
H. P. Ross.   *Richard Watson.
A. G. Olmsted.   Harman Yerkes.

BUTLER COUNTY.
Samuel Roberts . . . . April 30, 1803.
John Bredin . . . . April 18, 1831.
Daniel Agnew . . . . July 11, 1851.
Lawrence McGuffin.   A. L. Hazen.
E. McJunkin.   John McMichael.
James Bredin.   J. M. Greer.

CAMBRIA COUNTY.
George Taylor . . . . April 6, 1849.
John Dean.   Robert L. Johnston.
James Potts.   *A. V. Barker.

CAMERON COUNTY.
H. W. Williams . . . . March 29, 1865.
Stephen F. Wilson.
Arthur G. Olmsted.
*Charles A. Mayer.

CARBON COUNTY. (See MONROE.)

CENTRE COUNTY.
James Riddle . . . . February 24, 1794.
Jonathan Walker . . . . March 1, 1806.
Charles Huston . . . . July 1, 1818.
Thomas Burnside (Scottish) . . . . . . April 20, 1826.
*George W. Woodward . . . . April 9, 1841.
James Burnside . . . . April 20, 1853.
James Gamble . . . . July 15, 1859.
Samuel Linn . . . . November 5, 1859.
*J. B. McEnally.   *Adam Hoy.
*Charles A. Mayer.   *A. O. Furst.
*John H. Orvis.   J. G. Love.

CHESTER COUNTY.
John D. Coxe . . . . June 19, 1797.
*William Tilghman.
Bird Wilson (Scottish) . . . . March 1, 1806.

John Ross . . . . February 13, 1818.
*Isaac Darlington . . . . May 22, 1821.
Thomas S. Bell . . . . May 16, 1839.
John M. Forster . . . . November 18, 1846.
James Nill . . . . March 23, 1847.
*Henry Chapman . . . . March 18, 1848.
*Townsend Haines . . . . November 6, 1851.
*William Butler . . . . November 20, 1861.
William Futhey. *Thomas Butler.
W. B. Waddell. Joseph Hemphill.

CLARION COUNTY.

Alexander McCalmont . . . . May 31, 1839.
*Joseph Buffington . . . . June 1, 1849.
John C. Knox . . . . May 24, 1853.
G. W. Scofield . . . . July 6, 1861.
James Campbell . . . . November 20, 1861.
W. P. Jenks. Theophilus S. Wilson.
James B. Knox. W. W. Barr.
W. L. Corbett. E. H. Clark. (Scottish.)

CLEARFIELD COUNTY.

Charles Huston . . . . July 1, 1818.
Thomas Burnside (Scottish) . . . . April 20, 1826.
*George W. Woodward . . . . April 9, 1841.
James Burnside (Scottish) . . . . April 20, 1853.
James Gamble . . . . July 15, 1859.
Samuel Linn . . . . November 5, 1859.
*John H. Orvis. *David L. Krebs.
*Charles A. Mayer. Cyrus Gordon.

CLINTON COUNTY.

Thomas Burnside (Scottish) . . . . April 20, 1826.
*George W. Woodward . . . . April 9, 1841.
James Burnside (Scottish) . . . . April 20, 1826.
James Gamble . . . . July 15, 1859.
Samuel Linn . . . . November 5, 1859.
*John H. Orvis.
*Charles A. Mayer.

COLUMBIA COUNTY.

*Seth Chapman . . . . March 1, 1806.
Ellis Lewis . . . . October 14, 1833.
*Charles G. Donnel . . . . January 14, 1843.
*Joseph B. Anthony . . . . March 25, 1844.
*William Jessup . . . . April 6, 1849.
John N. Conyngham (Scottish) . . . . November 6, 1851.
*Warren J. Woodward . . . . May 19, 1856.
Aaron K. Peckham . . . . December 10, 1861.
*William Elwell . . . . November 4, 1862.
H. S. Hinckley.
E. R. Ikeler.

CRAWFORD COUNTY.

Jesse Moore . . . . April 5, 1803.
*Henry Shippen . . . . January 24, 1825.
Nathaniel B. Eldred . . . . March 23, 1839.
*Gaylord Church . . . . April 3, 1843.
John Galbraith . . . . November 6, 1851.
Rasselas Brown . . . . June 29, 1860.
S. P. Johnson.   *S. N. Pettis.
David Derrickson.   *Pearson Church.
J. P. Vincent.   J. J. Henderson.
*L. D. Wetmore.   Frank J. Thomas.
W. H. Lowrie.

CUMBERLAND COUNTY.

John Joseph Henry . . . . December 16, 1793.
James Hamilton . . . . March 1, 1806.
*Charles Smith . . . . March 27, 1819.
John Reed . . . . July 10, 1820.
Samuel Hepburn . . . . March 5, 1839.
Frederick Watts . . . . March 9, 1849.
James H. Graham.   *M. C. Herman.
B. F. Junkin.   W. F. Sadler.
Charles A. Barnett.   E. W. Biddle.

DAUPHIN COUNTY.

John Joseph Henry . . . . December 16, 1793.
*Amos Ellmaker . . . . July 3, 1815.
David Scott . . . . December 21, 1816.
Samuel D. Franks . . . . July 29, 1818.
Calvin Blythe . . . . February 1, 1830.
James M. Porter . . . . July 1, 1839.
*Anson V. Parsons . . . . July 18, 1840.
Nathaniel B. Eldred . . . . March 30, 1843.
*John J. Pearson . . . . April 7, 1849.
R. M. Henderson.
John W. Simonton.
John B. McPherson.

DELAWARE COUNTY.

John D. Coxe . . . . June 19, 1797.
Bird Wilson (Scottish) . . . . March 1, 1806.
John Ross . . . . February 13, 1818.
*Isaac Darlington . . . . May 22, 1821.
Thomas S. Bell . . . . May 16, 1839.
John M. Forster . . . . November 18, 1846.
James Nill . . . . March 23, 1847.
*Henry Chapman . . . . March 18, 1848.
*Townsend Haines . . . . November 6, 1851.
*William Butler . . . . November 20, 1861.
William Futhey.
*Thomas J. Clayton.

ELK COUNTY.

Alex. McCalmont . . . . May 31, 1839.
*George W. Woodward . . . . April 9, 1841.
*Joseph Buffington . . . . June 1, 1849.
James T. Hale . . . . April 10, 1851.
Robert G. White . . . . November 6, 1851.
W. D. Brown.
*Charles H. Noyes.
*Charles A. Mayer.

ERIE COUNTY.

David Clark.
Jesse Moore . . . . April 5, 1803.
*Henry Shippen . . . . January 24, 1825.
Nathaniel B. Eldred . . . . March 23, 1839.
*Gaylord Church . . . . April 3, 1843.
James Thompson.
John Galbraith . . . . November 6, 1851.
Rasselas Brown . . . . June 29, 1860.
S. P. Johnston.   William A. Galbraith.
David Derrickson.   *Frank Gunnison.
J. P. Vincent.   *Emory A. Walling.
*L. D. Wetmore.

FAYETTE COUNTY.

Alexander Addison (Scottish) . . . . August 17, 1791.
Thomas H. Baird . . . . October 19, 1818.
Nathaniel Ewing . . . . February 15, 1838.
Samuel A. Gilmore . . . . February 28, 1848.
James Lindsey . . . . November 20, 1861.
J. K. Ewing.   Nathaniel Ewing.
Edward Campbell.   *S. L. Mestrezat.
A. E. Willson.   *Edmund H. Reppert.
James Inghram.

FOREST COUNTY.

Alexander McCalmont . . . . May 31, 1839.
*Joseph Buffington . . . . June 1, 1849.
John C. Knox . . . . November 6, 1851.
John S. McCalmont . . . . May 24, 1853.
G. W. Scofield . . . . July 6, 1861.
James Campbell . . . . November 20, 1861.
W. P. Jenks.
W. D. Brown.
*Charles H. Noyes.

FRANKLIN COUNTY.

James Riddle . . . . February 24, 1794.
James Hamilton . . . . March 1, 1806.
*Charles Smith . . . . March 27, 1819.
John Reed . . . . July 10, 1820.

John Tod (Scottish) . . . . June 8, 1824.
Alex. Thompson . . . . June 25, 1827.
J. S. Black . . . . March 30, 1842.
F. M. Kimmel . . . . November 6, 1851.
James Nill . . . . November 20, 1861.
Alexander King.
D. W. Rowe.
John Stewart.

FULTON COUNTY.

Jeremiah S. Black . . . . March 30, 1842.
F. M. Kimmel . . . . November 6, 1851.
James Nill . . . . November 20, 1861.
Alexander King.   *William McClean.*
D. W. Rowe.   *S. McC. Swope.*
David Wills.

GREENE COUNTY.

Alexander Addison (Scottish) . . . . August 17, 1791.
Thomas H. Baird . . . . October 19, 1818.
Nathaniel Ewing . . . . February 15, 1839.
Samuel A. Gilmore . . . . February 28, 1848.
James Lindsey . . . . November 20, 1861.
J. K. Ewing.   *Nathaniel Ewing.*
A. E. Willson.   **S. L. Mestrezat.*
James Inghram.   *R. L. Crawford.*

HUNTINGDON COUNTY.

James Riddle . . . . February 24, 1794.
Jonathan Walker . . . . March 1, 1806.
Charles Huston . . . . July 1, 1818.
Thomas Burnside (Scottish) . . . . April 20, 1826.
*George W. Woodward.
George Taylor . . . . April 6, 1849.
John Dean.   *W. McK. Williamson.*
*Adam Hoy.   *J. M. Bailey.*
*A. O. Furst.

INDIANA COUNTY.

John Young . . . . March 1, 1806.
*Thomas White . . . . December 13, 1836.
Jeremiah M. Burrell . . . . March 25, 1847.
John C. Knox . . . . April 11, 1848.
*Joseph Buffington . . . . November 5, 1855.
J. A. Logan.
John P. Blair.
Harry White.

JEFFERSON COUNTY.

Thomas Burnside (Scottish).
Nathaniel B. Eldred . . . . November 10, 1835.
Alexander McCalmont . . . . May 31, 1839.
*Joseph Buffington . . . . June 1, 1849.
John C. Knox . . . . May 24, 1853.

G. W. Scofield . . . . July 6, 1861.
James Campbell . . . . November 20, 1861.
W. P. Jenks.   W. W. Barr.
James B. Knox.   E. H. Clark (Scottish).
W. L. Corbett.   John W. Reed.
Theophilus S. Wilson.

JUNIATA COUNTY.
John Reed.   B. F. Junkin.
Samuel Hepburn.   Charles A. Barnett.
Frederick Watts.   Jeremiah Lyons.
James H. Graham.

LACKAWANNA COUNTY.
*Garrick M. Harding.   *Thomas F. Connolly.
*John Handley.   *Frederick W. Gunster.
*Alfred Hand.   *Peter P. Smith.
Robert W. Archbald (Scottish).   *Henry M. Edwards.
*Henry M. Knapp.

LANCASTER COUNTY.
John Joseph Henry . . . . December 16, 1793.
*Walter Franklin . . . . January 18, 1811.
Charles Ogle . . . . April 1, 1836.
Oristus Collins . . . . December 27, 1838.
*Benjamin Champneys . . . . July 6, 1839.
Ellis Lewis (Scottish) . . . . January 14, 1843.
*H. G. Long . . . . November 6, 1854.
Alexander L. Hayes . . . . November 13, 1854.
J. B. Livingston.   David McMullen.
David W. Patterson.   D. C. Brubaker.

LAWRENCE COUNTY.
John Bredin . . . . February 28, 1842.
Daniel Agnew . . . . July 11, 1851.
Lawrence McGuffin.   John McMichael.
E. McJunkin.   John M. Greer.
James Bredin.   W. D. Wallace.
A. L. Hazen.

LEBANON COUNTY.
John Joseph Henry . . . . December 16, 1793.
*Amos Ellmaker . . . . July 3, 1815.
David Scott . . . . December 21, 1816.
Samuel D. Franks . . . . July 29, 1818.
Calvin Blythe . . . . February 1, 1830.
James M. Porter . . . . July 1, 1839.
*Anson V. Parsons . . . . July 16, 1840.
Nathaniel B. Eldred . . . . March 30, 1843.
*John J. Pearson . . . . April 7, 1849.
R. M. Henderson.   *F. E. Meily.
John W. Simonton.   A. W. Ehrgood.
John B. McPherson.

LEHIGH COUNTY.

*Jacob Rush . . . . August 17, 1793.
*John Spayd . . . . March 1, 1806.
Robert Porter . . . . July 6, 1809.
Garrick Mallory . . . . April 1, 1831.
John Banks . . . . April 1, 1836.
*J. Pringle Jones . . . . March 13, 1847.
Washington McCartney . . . . November 6, 1851.
Henry D. Maxwell . . . . July 21, 1856.
ᵣ *John K. Findlay* . . . . November 26, 1857.
*John W. Maynard . . . . November 7, 1862.
*A. B. Longaker.
*A. H. Meyers.
*Edward Albright.

LUZERNE COUNTY.

*Timothy Pickering.
*Jacob Rush . . . . August 17, 1793.
John B. Gibson . . . . October 14, 1812.
Thomas Burnside (Scottish) . . . . June 28, 1816.
David Scott . . . . July 7, 1818.
*William Jessup . . . . April 7, 1838.
John N. Conyngham (Scottish) . . . . November 6, 1851.
*E. L. Dana.   *Charles E. Rice.
*G. M. Harding.   *Stanley Woodward.
*John Handley.   John Lynch.
*D. L. Rhone.   *L. H. Bennett.
*W. H. Stanton.   A. Darte.

LYCOMING COUNTY.

*Jacob Rush . . . . August 17, 1793.
*Seth Chapman . . . . March 1, 1806.
Ellis Lewis (Scottish) . . . . October 14, 1833.
*Charles G. Donnel . . . . January 14, 1843.
*Joseph B. Anthony . . . . March 25, 1844.
James Pollock . . . . January 16, 1851.
*B. S. Bentley.   *H. H. Cummin.*
James Gamble.   *John J. Metzger.

McKEAN AND POTTER COUNTIES.

*Edward Herrick . . . . July 7, 1818.
Nathaniel B. Eldred . . . . November 10, 1835.
Alex. McCalmont . . . . May 31, 1839.
John N. Conyngham (Scottish) . . . . March 25, 1839.
*Horace Williston . . . . April 6, 1849.
Robert G. White . . . . November 6, 1851.
H. W. Williams . . . . March 29, 1865.
S. F. Wilson.
A. G. Olmsted.
Thomas A. Morrison.

MERCER COUNTY.

Jesse Moore	April 5, 1803.
John Bredin	April 18, 1831.
John C. Knox	November 6, 1851.
John S. McCalmont	May 24, 1853.
G. W. Scofield	July 6, 1861.
James Campbell	November 20, 1861.

W. P. Jenks. Arcus McDermitt.
I. G. Gordon. S. S. Mehard.
*John Trunkey. Samuel H. Miller.
William Maxwell.

MIFFLIN COUNTY.

James Riddle	February 24, 1794.
Jonathan Walker	March 1, 1806.
Charles Huston	July 1, 1818.
Thomas Burnside (Scottish)	April 20, 1826.
Abraham S. Wilson	March 30, 1842.
S. S. Woods	November 20, 1861.

*Joseph C. Bucher.
Harold M. McClure.
J. M. Bailey.

MONROE AND CARBON COUNTIES.

Nathaniel B. Eldred	April 6, 1849.
Luther Kidder.	
George R. Barrett	April 29, 1853.
James M. Porter	November 19, 1853.
Thomas S. Bell	March 23, 1855.

*Samuel S. Dreher.
*John B. Storm.
Allen Craig.

MONTGOMERY COUNTY.

John D. Coxe	June 19, 1797.
Bird Wilson (Scottish)	March 1, 1806.
John Ross	January 13, 1818.
*John Fox	April 16, 1830.
Thomas Burnside (Scottish)	March 30, 1841.
*David Krause	January 31, 1845.
*Daniel M. Smyser	November 6, 1851.

*Henry Chapman. *B. M. Boyer.
H. P. Ross. *A. S. Swartz.
*A. G. Olmsted. *H. G. Weand.
H. Stinson.

MONTOUR COUNTY.

James Pollock	January 16, 1851.
Alex. Jordan	November 6, 1851.

*W. M. Rockefeller.
H. S. Hinckley.
E. R. Ikeler.

NORTHAMPTON COUNTY.

*Jacob Rush . . . . August 17, 1793.
*John Spayd . . . . March 1, 1806.
Robert Porter . . . . July 6, 1809.
*Garrick Mallory . . . . April 1, 1831.
John Banks . . . . April 1, 1836.
*J. Pringle Jones . . . . March 31, 1847.
Washington McCartney . . . . November 6, 1851.
Henry D. Maxwell . . . . July 21, 1856.
John K. Findlay . . . . November 26, 1857.
*John W. Maynard . . . . November 7, 1862.
*A. B. Longaker.   *W. W. Schuyler.
*O. H. Meyers.   *H. J. Reeder.
W. S. Kirkpatrick.   *H. W. Scott.*

NORTHUMBERLAND COUNTY.

*Frederick Antes.
*Jacob Rush . . . . August 17, 1793.
*Seth Chapman . . . . March 1, 1806.
Ellis Lewis (Scottish) . . . . October 14, 1833.
*Charles G. Donnel . . . . January 14, 1843.
*Joseph B. Anthony . . . . March 25, 1844.
James Pollock . . . . January 16, 1851.
Alex. Jordan . . . . November 6, 1851.
*W. M. Rockefeller.
*C. R. Savidge.

PERRY COUNTY.

John Reed.   *B. F. Junkin.*
Samuel Hepburn.   *Charles A. Barnett.*
Frederick Watts.   *Jeremiah Lyons.*
James H. Graham.

PHILADELPHIA COUNTY.

PRESIDENT JUDGES (COMMON PLEAS, DISTRICT COURT, AND ORPHANS' COURT).

*James Biddle.   J. I. Clark Hare.
John D. Coxe.   *James R. Ludlow.*
*William Tilghman.   M. Russell Thayer.
*Jacob Rush.   William B. Hanna.
*John Hallowell.   Thomas K. Finletter.
Edward King.   *Craig Biddle.* (Scottish).
Oswald Thompson.   *Michael Arnold.
Joseph Allison.   Samuel W. Pennypacker.

ASSOCIATE LAW JUDGES.

Jonathan Bayard Smith.
William Robinson, Jr.
Isaac Howell.
Thomas L. Moore.
Joseph Redman.
Reynold Keen.
Jonathan Williams.
William Coats.
Edward W. Heston.
David Jackson.
John Inskeep.
Frederick Wolbert.
Jacob Franklin Heston.
*James Sharswood.
John Geyer.
Joseph Hemphill.
Anthony Simmons.
Jacob Sommer.
William Moulder.
Samuel Badger.
*Thomas Sergeant.
Thomas Armstrong.
Joseph Borden McKean.
George W. Morgan.
George Morton.
Edward Duffield Ingraham.
Hugh Ferguson.
*Jared Ingersoll.
Benjamin R. Morgan.
Joseph Barnes.
Charles S. Coxe.
Jonathan T. Knight.
*Anson V. Parsons.
Robert J. Conrad.
Joel B. Sutherland.
Archbald Randall.

George M. Stroud.
Thomas McKean Pettit.
Roberts Vaux.
John Richter Jones.
James Campbell.
John K. Findlay.
Joel Jones.
William D. Kelley.
*George Sharswood.
William S. Peirce.
Frederick Carroll Brewster.
Thomas Greenbank.
*Edward M. Paxson.
James Lynd.
*James T. Mitchell.
Amos Briggs.
Joseph T. Pratt.
Thomas R. Elcock.
D. Newlin Fell.
W. H. Yerkes.
Theodore B. Dwight.
Dennis W. O'Brien.
*William N. Ashman.
Clement B. Penrose. (Scottish.)
Robert M. Willson.
James Gay Gordon.
*F. A. Brégy.
Henry Reed.
Joseph C. Ferguson.
Theodore F. Jenkins.
Abraham M. Beitler.
*Mayer Sulzberger.
William W. Wiltbank. (Scottish.)
Charles B. McMichael.
Charles F. Audenreid.

PIKE COUNTY.

John B. Gibson . . . . October 14, 1812.
Thomas Burnside (Scottish) . . . . June 28, 1816.
David Scott . . . . July 7, 1818.
Nathaniel B. Eldred . . . . April 6, 1849.
George R. Barrett . . . . April 29, 1853.
James M. Porter . . . . November 19, 1853.
Thomas S. Bell . . . . March 23, 1855.
*Samuel S. Dreher.   Henry M. Seeley.
Charles P. Waller.   *George S. Purdy.

POTTER COUNTY. (See McKEAN.)

SCHUYLKILL COUNTY.

Robert Porter.
*Amos Ellmaker . . . . July 3, 1815.
David Scott . . . . December 21, 1816.
Samuel D. Franks . . . . July 29, 1818.
Calvin Blythe . . . . February 1, 1830.
Luther Kidder . . . . October 23, 1844.
*C. W. Hegins . . . . November 6, 1851.
*Edward Owen Parry.   *D. B. Green.
James Ryon.   O. P. Bechtel.
*C. L. Pershing.   Mason Weidman.
*Henry Souther.   P. M. Dunn.
T. H. Walker.   *Richard Koch.

SNYDER COUNTY.

Abraham S. Wilson . . . . March 30, 1842.
S. S. Woods . . . . November 20, 1861.
*Joseph C. Bucher.
Harold M. McClure.

SOMERSET COUNTY.

Bernard Dougherty.
George Woods.
James Riddle . . . . February 24, 1794.
Thomas H. Baird . . . . October 19, 1818.
John Tod (Scottish) . . . . June 8, 1824.
Alex. Thompson . . . . June 25, 1827.
Jeremiah S. Black . . . . March 30, 1842.
F. M. Kimmel . . . . November 6, 1851.
James Nill . . . . November 20, 1861.
Alexander King.   *W. J. Baer.
D. W. Rowe.   *J. H. Longenecker.
William Maclay Hall.

SULLIVAN COUNTY.

*Charles G. Donnel . . . . January 14, 1843.
*Joseph B. Anthony . . . . March 25, 1844.
*Horace Williston . . . . April 6, 1849.
David Wilmot . . . . November 6, 1851.
*Warren J. Woodward . . . . May 19, 1856.
A. K. Peckham . . . . December 10, 1861.
*William Elwell . . . . November 4, 1862.
T. J. Ingham.
*John A. Sittser.
*E. A. Dunham.

SUSQUEHANNA COUNTY.

John B. Gibson.
Thomas Burnside.
Edward Herrick . . . . July 7, 1818.
William Jessup . . . . April 7, 1838.
John N. Conyngham (Scottish) . . . . . . March 25, 1839.

David Wilmot . . . . November 6, 1851.
Darius Bullock . . . . August 8, 1857.
Ulysses Mercur . . . . March 19, 1861.
Ferris B. Streater . . . . March 4, 1865.
W. H. Jessup.
J. B. McCollum.
D. W. Searle.

TIOGA COUNTY.
John B. Gibson.
Thomas Duncan.
*Edward Herrick . . . . July 7, 1818.
John N. Conyngham (Scottish) . . . . . . March 25, 1839.
*Horace Williston . . . . April 6, 1849.
Robert G. White . . . . November 6, 1851.
H. W. Williams . . . . March 29, 1865.
Stephen F. Wilson.
John I. Mitchell.

UNION COUNTY.
*Seth Chapman . . . . March 1, 1806.
Ellis Lewis . . . . October 14, 1833.
Abraham S. Wilson . . . . March 30, 1842.
S. S. Woods . . . . November 20, 1861.
*Joseph C. Bucher.
Harold M. McClure.

VENANGO COUNTY.
Alex. Addison. (Scottish.)
Jesse Moore . . . . April 5, 1803.
*Henry Shippen . . . . January 24, 1825.
Alexander McCalmont . . . . May 31, 1839.
Nathaniel B. Eldred.
*Gaylord Church.
*Joseph Buffington . . . . June 1, 1849.
John C. Knox . . . . May 24, 1853.
John G. McCalmont.
G. W. Scofield . . . . July 6, 1861.
James Campbell . . . . November 20, 1861.
Isaac G. Gordon.   Charles E. Taylor.
*John Trunkey.   George S. Criswell.

WARREN COUNTY.
S. P. Johnston.   *L. D. Wetmore.
David Derrickson.   W. D. Brown.
J. P. Vincent.   *Charles H. Noyes.

WAYNE COUNTY.
*Jacob Rush . . . . August 17, 1793.
John B. Gibson . . . . October 14, 1812.
Thomas Burnside (Scottish) . . . . June 28, 1816.

David Scott . . . . July 7, 1818.
Nathaniel B. Eldred . . . . April 6, 1849.
George R. Barrett . . . . April 29, 1853.
James M. Porter . . . . November 19, 1853.
Thomas S. Bell . . . . March 23, 1855.
*S. S. Dreher.   Henry M. Seeley.
C. P. Waller.   *George S. Purdy.

WASHINGTON COUNTY.
*Henry Taylor.
Alex. Addison. (Scottish.)
Samuel Roberts.
Thomas H. Baird . . . . October 19, 1818.
Nathaniel Ewing . . . . February 15, 1838.
Samuel A. Gilmore . . . . February 28, 1848.
James Lindsay.
J. K. Ewing.
B. B. Chamberlain . . . . February 3, 1866.
A. W. Acheson . . . . November 15, 1866.
George S. Hart.
J. A. McIlvaine.
*James F. Taylor.

WESTMORELAND COUNTY.
John Moore.
Alexander Addison (Scottish) . . . . August 17, 1791.
John Young (Scottish) . . . . March 1, 1806.
*Thomas White . . . . December 13, 1836.
Jeremiah N. Burrell . . . . March 25, 1847.
John C. Knox . . . . April 11, 1848.
Joseph Buffington . . . . November 5, 1855.
J. A. Logan.   *L. W. Doty.*
James A. Hunter.   *A. D. McConnell.*

WYOMING COUNTY.
*William Jessup . . . . April 7, 1838.
John N. Conyngham (Scottish) . . . . . . November 6, 1851.
*Warren J. Woodward . . . . May 19, 1856.
A. K. Peckham . . . . December 10, 1861.
*William Elwell . . . . November 4, 1862.
T. J. Ingham.
*John A. Sittser.
*E. A. Dunham.

YORK COUNTY.
John Joseph Henry . . . . December 16, 1793.
*Walter Franklin . . . . January 18, 1811.
*Daniel Durkee . . . . May 4, 1835.
William N. Irvine . . . . February 6, 1846.
*Robert J. Fisher.   *J. W. Latimer.*
P. L. Wickes.   *J. W. Bittenger.*
John Gibson.   *W. F. B. Stewart.*

APPENDIX B.

The following lists contain nearly all the names given in Appendix A, but now arranged in alphabetical order. Italics mean Scottish or Scotch-Irish descent in some degree; a star means that such descent is lacking; roman type without a star means that no information has been obtained. The authority for assigning a name to a particular class is usually given. In some instances, however, a name is assigned without giving any authority. In these cases the conclusion was reached either by Dr. William H. Egle, State Librarian, or by Major William C. Armor, of Harrisburg, both well known for their antiquarian and genealogical studies, who were kind enough to put their knowledge at my disposal and to assist me also by the examination of local histories and biographical sketches. If the same person was successively upon the bench of the common pleas and one of the appellate courts, his name will be found only in the appellate lists.

JUDGES UNDER THE COMMONWEALTH.

COURT OF ADMIRALTY.

*Hopkinson, Francis.
Ross, George.

HIGH COURT OF ERRORS AND APPEALS UNDER ACT OF FEBRUARY 28, 1780.

*Atlee, William Augustus.
*Bayard, James.
Bryan, George.
*Dickinson, John.
*Evans, John.
*Franklin, Benjamin.
*Hopkinson, Francis.
McKean, Thomas.
*Mifflin, Thomas.
Miles, Samuel.
Moore, William.
Reed, Joseph.
*Rush, Jacob.
*Shippen, Edward.
Smith, James.
*Wynkoop, Henry.

As Reorganized, Act of April 13, 1791.

Addison, Alexander.
  Judge Addison was born in Ireland and educated at Edinburgh, Scotland. He was the editor of Addison's Reports. For further facts see Judge White's paper in *Pennsylvania Historical Magazine*, vol. VII., No. 2.

*Atlee, William Augustus.
*Biddle, James.
 Brackenridge, Hugh Henry.
 Bradford, William.
*Chew, Benjamin.
 Coxe, John D.
 Henry, John Joseph.
 McKean, Thomas.
 Riddle, James.
*Rush, Jacob.
*Shippen, Edward.
 Smith, Thomas.
*Tilghman, William.
*Yeates, Jasper.

CHIEF JUSTICES OF THE SUPREME COURT.

Agnew, Daniel.
  Member Pennsylvania Scotch-Irish Society.

Black, Jeremiah S.
  On the authority of Dr. Egle, Judges Martin Bell, of Blair, and John Stewart, of Franklin. Judge Longenecker, of Bedford, says: "Judge Black's great grandfather came from the North of Ireland. His mother was Mary Sullivan, the daughter of Patrick Sullivan, who, I need not say, was an Irishman."

Gibson, John Bannister.
  Justices Mitchell and Williams and Dr. Egle.

Gordon, Isaac G.
  Justice Williams.

Lewis, Ellis.
  His daughter, Josephine Lewis, writes as follows: "My father, Judge Lewis, was of Welsh descent; but his grandmother, Ruth Wilson, daughter of John Wilson, was of Scotch parentage. I think her mother, Ruth Hind, was of Irish birth. This is the only Scotch or Irish strain in the family that I know of."

Lowrie, Walter H.
  Justice Williams and Judge Thomas, of Crawford. See also paper by Judge J. W. F. White, of Allegheny, *Pennsylvania Historical Magazine*, vol. VII., No. 2.

McKean, Thomas.
  Justices Williams and Mitchell.

*Mercur, Ulysses.
  German; so stated by his son, Rodney A. Mercur, of Towanda.

*Paxson, Edward M.
  English Quaker; Justice Williams.

*Read, John Meredith.
  English and Welsh; so stated by his son, John Meredith Read; reported by Justice Mitchell.

*Reed, Joseph. (Declined.)
  Justice Mitchell.

*Sharswood, George.
  English; Justice Mitchell.

*Shippen, Edward.
    English; Justice Mitchell.
Sterrett, James P.
    Member Pennsylvania Scotch-Irish Society.
Thompson, James.
    His son, former Justice Samuel G. Thompson, writes: "My father on both sides was of Scotch-Irish descent, and in many of his characteristics typified in a strong way his race."
*Tilghman, William.
    English; Justice Mitchell.
*Woodward, George W.
    Judge Stanley Woodward, of Luzerne.

ASSOCIATE JUSTICES OF THE SUPREME COURT.

Armstrong, James.
*Atlee, William Augustus.
Bell, Thomas S.
    Judge Hemphill, of Chester.
Brackenridge, Hugh Henry.
    Scottish; Justice Mitchell and Dr. Egle.
*Bradford, William.
    English; Justice Mitchell.
Bryan, George.
    Justice Mitchell.
Burnside, Thomas.
    Scottish; so stated by his daughter, Mrs. Morris; reported by Justice Mitchell; also by Judges Love, of Centre; Swartz, of Montgomery; and Yerkes, of Bucks.
Chambers, George.
    Justice Williams.
*Church, Gaylord.
    English; James Sill, of Erie.
Clark, Silas M.
    Justice Williams and Judge Harry White, of Indiana.
Coulter, Richard.
Dean, John.
    Judge Bell.
Duncan, Thomas.
    Justice Williams.
*Evans, John.
    Probably Welsh; Justice Mitchell.
*Fell, D. Newlin,
    Writes: "My ancestors came from the extreme northwest part of England, close to the west coast and to the southern boundary of Scotland. Judge Trunkey's mother was a Fell, and his line on one side is the same as mine."
*Green, Henry,
    Answers, "No."
*Hand, Alfred.
    New England. See Kulp's "Families of the Wyoming Valley."

*Heydrick, Christopher.
    Dutch; Justice Williams.
Huston, Charles.
    Dr. Egle, J. Simpson Africa, of Huntingdon, and Judge Love.
Kennedy, John.
    Justice Williams. He was a great grandfather of Nathaniel K. Ewing, lately upon the bench of Fayette County.
Knox, John C.
    Justice Williams and Judges Doty, of Westmoreland, and Reed, of Jefferson.
McCollum, J. Brewster.
    Member of Pennsylvania Scotch-Irish Society.
*Mitchell, James T.,
    Writes: "I am not of Scotch-Irish ancestry. My maternal grandfather was Irish by birth, but of English descent from an officer in Cromwell's army."
Porter, William A.
    His son, Judge William W. Porter, of the Superior Court, writes: "My grandfather was David R. Porter; my great grandfather was Gen. Andrew Porter; my great great grandfather was Robert Porter, who emigrated from what is known as the Isle of Bird, about nine miles from Londonderry, in 1720."
Rodgers, Molton Cropper.
Ross, John.
    Judge Yerkes, of Bucks.
*Rush, Jacob.
*Sergeant, Thomas.
    English; Justice Mitchell.
Smith, Frederick.
Smith, Thomas.
Strong, William.
Thompson, Samuel Gustine.
    See Thompson, James, *supra.*
Tod, John.
    Scottish; on the authority of his daughter, Mrs. John H. Briggs, of Harrisburg. Judge Longenecker says: "Tod was a Connecticut man, graduated at Yale, and came at once to Bedford. He arrived here about 1800. One of his daughters married John H. Briggs, of Harrisburg, and another married William Kerr, of the same place."
*Trunkey, John.
    See Fell, D. Newlin, *supra.*
*Williams, Henry W. (of Allegheny).
    New England; Judge Kennedy, of Allegheny. See also Judge White's paper.
Williams, Henry W. (of Tioga).
    President Pennsylvania Scotch-Irish Society, 1898. He writes: "I am Scotch-Irish by a paternal grandmother, who was a Grant."
*Woodward, Warren J.
    English; Judge Endlich, of Berks.
*Yeates, Jasper.
    English; Justice Mitchell.

JUDGES OF THE SUPERIOR COURT.

*Beaver, James A.,
Writes: "So far as blood is concerned, I have nearly everything known to the early settlement of Pennsylvania in my veins excepting Scotch-Irish. I am largely from the Palatinate, a little mixture of French, and considerable of English, and, possibly, of Welsh, but no Scotch-Irish. At a meeting of the Scotch-Irish Society of Pittsburgh some time ago I claimed relationship on the ground that I inherited my Scotch-Irish blood through my children. They have plenty of it of the most pronounced sort, coming from Hugh McAllister, who came in 1736, and whose son, Major Hugh, was a noted character in many ways in Indian campaigns and during the Revolution."

Orlady, George B.,
Writes: "I can state on the authority of my mother, who yet enjoys perfect health at seventy-eight years of age, that on her side of the house the ancestry is as absolutely Scotch-Irish as it can well be, through the Shannons, Campbells, Caldwells, and Boals as forebears."

Porter, William D.,
Answers, "Yes."

Porter, William W.
Member Pennsylvania Scotch-Irish Society. See Porter, William, *supra.*

*Reeder, Howard J.

*Rice, Charles E.,
Answers, "No."

*Smith, Peter P.,
Writes: "I am of Irish ancestry wholly, so far as the family history and tradition disclose."

Wickham, John J.,
Writes: "In the direct line my ancestors were English, settled in Ireland; at least the main stems had their roots in England. I am related, however, to Scotch-Irish Presbyterian families in the North of Ireland, but I have never taken the time to ascertain how the relationship arose."

*Willard, Edward N.,
Writes: "My father was a Yankee, my mother was a Yankee, and I am a Yankee. I think there is no Scotch-Irish blood in my veins."

JUDGES OF THE COMMON PLEAS AND ORPHANS' COURT.

Acheson, A. W.
Judge McIlvaine, of Washington, Pa., writes: "His father came to Washington from County Armagh, Ireland."

*Albright, Edward,
Writes that he is of German descent.

Allison, Joseph,
Was a member of Pennsylvania Scotch-Irish Society.

*Antes, Frederick.
George D. Snyder, city engineer of Williamsport, Pa., writes: "He was of German parentage on both sides."

*Anthony, Joseph B.
C. Larue Munson, of Williamsport, Pa., who married a granddaughter—Josephine Anthony White—furnishes the following information: "George Anthony was born in Strasburg, Germany, and settled in Pennsylvania in 17 . His son William was born in 1765 and died in 1831. William's wife, Martha Biles, who was born in 1767 and died in 1848, was the daughter of Alexander Biles, of Maidenhead, England. Judge Anthony was the son of William and Martha. He was born in Philadelphia, June 19th, 1795, graduated with high honors from Princeton College, and then came to Williamsport, where he was admitted to the bar in 1818. Within a very short time he secured a leading position in his profession, becoming a very successful and distinguished lawyer. He was also famed for his wit and anecdotes, and, possessing high social qualities and a pleasing manner, easily made and kept many friends. In 1830 he was elected to the State senate, and served until 1833, when he was chosen to congress, and again in 1835. At this election he had the unequaled good fortune to carry every election precinct in every county composing his congressional district. After his second term in congress expired he was appointed by Governor Porter judge of the Nicholson Court, organized to settle the title to vast tracts of valuable land. and in 1844 was made president judge of the eighth judicial district. He died January 10th, 1851."

Archbald, Robert W.,
Writes: "My father was born in Scotland and my mother was of New England descent. I had an uncle Patrick, which has an Irish flavor about it, but Patrick is as Scotch as it is Irish. St. Patrick, as you know, was a Scot, and his adoption as the patron saint of the Emerald Isle is the original Irish bull. * * * My father's family used to live in the Little Cumry Islands, which is a distinctively Welsh name, and I am able to blend Scotch, Irish, and Welsh. * * * Some of my father's mother's family undoubtedly crossed the Channel and had a permanent residence in Ireland. But, candidly speaking, I have no claim to be among the Scotch-Irish people who played such an important part in the development of Pennsylvania." An excellent claim would probably be raised upon these facts, but at least there is no doubt about Judge Archbald's Scottish descent. .

Armstrong, Thomas.

*Arnold, Michael,
Writes: "My ancestors on both sides were German."

*Ashman, William N.,
Answers, "No."

Audenried, Charles F.,
Writes: "I am partly of Scotch-Irish blood, despite my German name. My maternal grandmother was a Miss Wills, of Dauphin County, and her mother was of the Wallace family. The Audenrieds came from Wurtemberg originally, and my mother's family are almost pure Welsh blood."

Badger, Samuel.

*Baer, W. J.
German; so stated by him to Judge Longenecker, of Bedford.

Bailey, John H.
Judge W. D. Porter, of Allegheny.

Bailey, J. M.,
    Answers, "Yes."

Baird, Thomas H.
    Judge Crawford and A. A. Purman, of Waynesburg, Greene County. Judge McIlvaine also writes: "Thomas H. Baird was a grandson of one John Baird, a Scotchman, who came to America with Braddock's army."

Banks, John.
    Judge Endlich, of Berks.

*Barker, A. V.,
    Writes that he is of Puritan descent.

Barnes, Joseph.

Barnett, Charles A.

Barr, W. W.,
    Who sends the following: "David Barr, the grandfather of the subject of this sketch, on the father's side, came from the North of Ireland about the year 1770. Settled first in Mifflin County, Pennsylvania, and shortly afterwards removed to Centre County; was a soldier in the Continental army for a time. David Semple, the grandfather on the mother's side, came from about the same place a little time later and settled in Huntingdon County. These old men were about the same age and were both Scotch-Irish Presbyterians, and lived to be over eighty years of age. William Barr, the father, was born on his father's farm, in Penn's Valley, Centre County, in the year 1794; he was married to Jane Semple in 1816, and W. W. Barr was born on the same farm, 1827, February 15th. In early life lived on the farm and attended the common schools; afterwards he went to school at Dickinson Seminary, at Williamsport. In 1850 he commenced the study of law in the office of Joseph Alexander, Esq., at Lewistown, Pa., and was admitted to the bar in 1852. In 1853 he removed to Clarion, Pa., and commenced the practice of the law at that place, and has resided there ever since. In 1852 and 1853 he was a transcribing clerk in the House of Representatives at Harrisburg. In 1854 he was elected district attorney for Clarion County, and in 1857 was re-elected to the same office. In 1861 he was elected treasurer of Clarion County. In 1864 was elected a member of the General Assembly of Pennsylvania, and in 1865 was re-elected to the same. In 1879 was again elected district attorney of Clarion County, and in 1882 was re-elected the same, serving in all twelve years in this office. In 1891, on the death of Hon. T. S. Wilson, he was appointed by Governor Pattison president judge of the eighteenth judicial district of Pennsylvania, comprising Clarion County, with Jefferson attached. Also in 1868, 1869, and 1890 he was District Deputy Grand Master of the Masons for the District of Venango, Clarion, Armstrong, Indiana, and Cambria Counties."

Barrett, George R.

*Beitler, Abraham M.,
    Writes: "I think I am Dutch or German for several generations back."

Bechtel, Oliver P.,
    Writes: "As to myself, from my father's side there is Scotch-Irish through the family known by us as the Bryan-McCool family."

Bell, Martin,
   Answers, "Yes."
*Bennett, Lyman H.,
   Answers "No. Probably of New England descent."
*Bentley, Benjamin S.
   New England; C. Larue Munson.
Biddle, Craig,
   Writes: "My maternal grandfather, John Craig, was the son of a Scotchman. My maternal grandmother, whose maiden name was Margaret M. Craig, was the daughter of an Irishman."
Biddle, Edward W.,
   Answers, "Yes."
*Biddle, James.
   Judge Craig Biddle writes: "James Biddle (1731–1797) was president judge of the First Judicial District in 1791, and was of English ancestry, not Scotch or Irish."
Bittinger, John W.,
   Writes: "My great grandfather, John Wierman, on my mother's side, was married to Ruth Cox, of Adams County, of Scotch-Irish descent. This is all the honor I can lay claim to in this direction, but in Pennsylvania-German I am great."
Blair, John P.
*Bland, Henry W.,
   Answers, "No."
Blythe, Calvin.
Boggs, Jackson.
*Boyer, B. M.
   German; Judge Swartz, of Montgomery.
Bredin, James.
   Judge Miller, of Mercer.
Bredin, John.
   Judge Greer, of Butler, thinks he was born in Ireland and came to America in infancy.
*Brégy, F. Amédeé,
   Answers, "No."
Brewster, Frederick Carroll.
Briggs, Amos.
*Brown, Rasselas.
   New England; James Sill, of Erie.
Brown, W. D.
   Judge Noyes, late of Warren.
Brubaker, Henry C.,
   Writes: "My paternal grandmother was Mary Devlin, whose parents were born in Northern Ireland."
Bucher, Joseph C.
*Buffington, Joseph.
   His nephew, Judge Buffington, of Kittanning, now on the Federal bench for the Western Pennsylvania District, writes: "To your question I will have to answer no. * * * He was a lineal descendant of the first born child of English descent in the Province of Pennsylvania."

*Bullock, Darius.
    New England ; Rodney A. Mercur, of Towanda.
Burnside, James.
    Scottish ; Judge Love, of Centre.
Burrell, Jeremiah N.
    Judges Doty and McConnell, of Westmoreland.
*Butler, William.
*Butler, Thomas.
    These are father and son, and are of English ancestry, on the authority of Judge Hemphill, of Chester.
Campbell, Edward.
    Member of Pennsylvania Scotch-Irish Society.
Campbell, James.
    Judge Reed, of Jefferson.
Chamberlain, B. B.
    Judge McIlvaine writes: " B. B. Chamberlain was of Beaver County, and, I am informed, was of Scotch-Irish descent."
*Champneys, Benjamin.
    English descent; Samuel Evans, of Columbia.
*Chapman, Henry.
*Chapman, Seth.
    Arthur Chapman, of Doylestown, writes: " Henry Chapman was not of Scotch-Irish descent, either in the paternal or maternal line. He was not a near relative of Seth Chapman, although they were both descendants of the first settler, John Chapman."
    Judge Yerkes writes : " Judge Henry Chapman was a descendant of one of the first English settlers, but his mother was a Meredith, a relative of William M. Meredith. Were the Merediths Scotch ?"
*Church, Pearson.
    English ; James Sill.
Clark, David.
    James Sill writes: " Unadvised as I am as to Judge David Clark, both his Christian and surname induce the surmise that he was Scotch or Scotch-Irish, and the character or race of the settlers of Western Pennsylvania, over whom he was placed for life, adds weight to this."
Clark, E. Heath.
    Judge Clark writes as follows: " I am the only living son of Jesse G. Clark and Sarah W. Clark. I was born on July 22d, 1839 (am now in my fifty-ninth year), in Brookville, Jefferson County, Pennsylvania, where I continued to reside until I took my seat as president judge of Clarion county, with Jefferson county attached, then constituting the eighteenth judicial district, when I moved to Clarion, my present residence. My grandparents on my father's side were William and Susanna Clark, formerly Griffith. William Clark was born February 19th, 1791; Susan Griffith, February 27th, 1796. They were married in Cumberland county, Pennsylvania. They removed from there at an early date to Indiana county, and in the early years of the '30's moved to Brookville, Pa. He, Grandfather Clark, was elected sheriff in Jefferson county, and served one term. Grandfather Clark died January 13th, 1844, and his wife died January 31st,

1862. Grandfather Clark's father was a Scotchman. As to the Griffiths, I know nothing about their ancestry. On my mother's side of the house my grandparents were Thomas Hastings and Elizabeth Hastings, formerly Wagner. Thomas Hastings was born in Centre county, Pennsylvania, October 24th, 1797. He was elected sheriff of Centre county, Pennsylvania, in 1824, and was a member of the Assembly in 1827-28. He removed to Jefferson county in 1831 and was appointed prothonotary by Governor Wolf in 1832, and in 1837 was elected to the Constitutional Convention. In 1838, in connection with his son Capt. John Hastings, he established a newspaper called the *Backwoodsman*. He retired in two years from the paper in favor of his two sons, John and B. T. Hastings. In 1846 Governor Shunk appointed him associate judge of Jefferson county. He and his wife celebrated the fiftieth anniversary of their married life June 5th, 1867. He died at Brookville in 1871, and his wife died within a few years after. All I know as to the Hastings, they were said to be of English descent. My father, Jesse G. Clark, was admitted to the Jefferson county bar about May, 1838. A short time prior thereto he was elected and served as county treasurer. He was the law partner of D. Barclay Jenks, a brother of the Hon. William P. Jenks and Hon. George A. Jenks, during the year 1841. Father died February 4th, 1847.

"I was admitted to the Jefferson county bar in 1866, being at that time a student at law under the firm of said W. P. and George A. Jenks. About 1869 I became a law partner of theirs, and the firm was known as Jenks, Jenks & Clark. In 1871 William P. Jenks was elected president judge of the eighteenth judicial district, and served out the full term. I continued the practice of law with Hon. George A. Jenks for about twenty years. He, during the continuance of our partnership, was appointed Assistant Secretary of the Interior under President Cleveland, and afterwards was appointed Solicitor-General."

*Clayton, Thomas J.,
Writes: "None of my ancestors are of Scotch-Irish descent. We are all 'bloody' English from the town of Clayton, in Sussex, and from the city of York. My wife is of Scotch-Irish descent. She was a McCay or MacKay."

Coates, William.

*Collier, Frederick H.,
Writes: "I am of English and Pennsylvania-German ancestry."

Collins, Oristus.
Samuel Evans.

*Connolly, Thomas F.
Irish; Judge Archbald.

Conrad, Robert J.

Conyngham, John N.
Scottish; Judge Searle, of Wyoming, and Judge Stanley Woodward, of Luzerne.

Corbett, William L.
Judge Clark furnishes the following information: "His great grandparents were Donald C. and Mary Corbett; his grandparents were William and Sarah Corbett; his parents were Isaac and Margaret Corbett; his great grandmother, Mary Todd, was Scotch-Irish." The following sketch of Judge Corbett is taken from the memorial adopted by the Clarion county bar upon his death, in

April, 1895: "The subject of this memorial was born in Clarion township, near the borough of Clarion, on the twelfth day of February, 1826. He received his education in the common schools and the Clarion Academy. Studied law with D. W. Foster, Esq., and was admitted to the Clarion county bar February 2d, 1847. By study and close attention to business he soon acquired a reputation and a good practice at the bar. Judge Corbett in early life was a Whig in politics, but in 1854 he attached himself to the Democratic party, and on several occasions was chosen a delegate to county and State conventions. In 1868 he was a delegate to the Democratic national convention that nominated Horatio Seymour for president. In 1872 he was elected a delegate at large to the state constitutional convention, and served on the judiciary committee during the sittings of that body. In 1876 he was elected a member of the state senate of Pennsylvania, and served two years. In January, 1885, he was appointed president judge of the eighteenth judicial district by Governor Pattison to fill the vacancy caused by the death of Hon. James B. Knox, and served during that year."

*Coxe, Charles S.
 English; Judge Arnold.

Coxe, John D.

Craig, Allen,
 Writes: "My great grandfather came, as near as I can tell, from the North of Ireland. In the 'History of Lehigh and Carbon Counties,' doubtless in the State Library, you will find an article giving full information of my forefathers, under the title of Col. John Craig, a brother of mine."

Crawford, R. L.,
 Answers, "Yes."

Criswell, George S.,
 Writes: "My father's people have long been residents of Eastern Pennsylvania, my father coming to this county (Franklin) from Mifflin county about 1833. While I have no reliable data, I think the family is of English descent. My mother's people (Nickles) came to Centre county from the North of Ireland about the beginning of the present century, and, being Presbyterians, I presume they can be properly classed as Scotch-Irish."

Cummin, Hugh H.
 C. Larue Munson.

Dallas, Trevanian B.
 Scottish; Judge White of Allegheny.

*Dana, E. L.
 Probably of New England descent.

Darlington, Isaac.
 New England; Judge Hemphill.

Darte, A.

*Derrickson, David.
 Probably of New England descent; James Sill.

*Donnel, Charles G.

Doty, Lucien W.,
 Answers, "Yes."

Daugherty, Bernard.
    Judge Longenecker.
*Dreher, Samuel S.
    Pennsylvania-German; C. B. Staples, of Stroudsburg.
*Dunham, E. A.,
    Writes: "I suppose my ancestors to have been English and German."
Dunn, P. M.
*Durkee, Daniel.
    Judge Bittinger writes: "He was from Vermont, and his biographer calls him of English descent."
*Edwards, Henry M.
    Welsh.
Ehrgood, Allen W.,
    Writes: "My paternal grandmother was Scotch-Irish."
*Elcock, Thomas R.
    Irish; Judge Audenried.
*Eldred, Nathaniel B.
    New England; James Sill.
*Ellmaker, Amos.
    Samuel Evans, of Columbia, writes: "Amos Ellmaker was of German descent, and was born near New Holland, in this (Lancaster) county. He was admitted to the bar about 1809. He moved to Reading, was appointed Attorney-General, and moved to Harrisburg, and was afterwards appointed judge. He was not a brilliant lawyer, but careful and painstaking. At one time he controlled about two-thirds of the Orphans' Court practice in this county. He was only about sixty-two years old when he died. He married a daughter of Thomas Elder (Scotch Irish)."
*Elwell, William.
    George E. Elwell, of Bloomsburg, writes: "My father's ancestry is English. The first of his line is Robert Elwell, who came from Staffordshire, England, and located at Salem, Va., prior to 1635, and died May 18th, 1683. On his mother's side the line began with Captain Thomas Prentice, who settled in Newton Centre, Mass., about 1630. He served in Cromwell's army, so you see father is all English. On my mother's side we are chock full of Scotch-Irish, but that is not in question."
*Endlich, Gustav A.
    German, on his own authority.
*Ermentrout, James N.
    German, on his own authority.
Ewing, Nathaniel.
Ewing, J. Kennedy.
Ewing, Nathaniel, Jr.
    These are grandfather, father, and son. Nathaniel Ewing, Jr., is a member of the Pennsylvania Scotch-Irish Society. Judge McIlvaine writes: "Nathaniel Ewing's ancestors were Scotch-Irish. They emigrated from the North of Ireland to Maryland in the early part of the last century. * * * J. Kennedy Ewing was a son of Nathaniel Ewing and father of Nathaniel Ewing, Jr., who has just retired from the bench in Fayette County."

Ewing, Thomas.
    Member Pennsylvania Scotch-Irish Society.
Ferguson, Hugh.
Ferguson, Joseph C.,
    Writes: "I am of Scotch-Irish ancestry, both of my parents having been born in County Tyrone. They came to this country when very young, and married here." Judge Ferguson is a member of the Pennsylvania Scotch-Irish Society.
*Fetterman, C. S.
    Judge Kennedy, of Allegheny.
Findlay, John K.
Finletter, Thomas K.,
    Writes: "My father and mother were Scotch-Irish, as were all their progenitors. My wife's progenitors were the same, so that my children are Scotch-Irish of the purest blood." Member Pennsylvania Scotch-Irish Society.
*Fisher, Robert J.
    Judge Bittinger writes: "He was partly of Welsh descent, his middle name being Jones." Judge Latimer, of York, says he was not Scotch-Irish.
Forster, John M.
Forward, Walter.
    Chauncey F. Black, of York, writes as follows: "We have no knowledge of the Forward family on the other side of the water. We find them settled in Connecticut, where Walter Forward and his distinguished brothers were born—sons of one Samuel Forward, my great grandfather. The late W. Stump Forwood, of Maryland, made some investigations which convinced him that Forwood and Forward were the same names used by different branches of the family. In the course of his researches he learned that there was a very distinguished member of the Irish Parliament named Forward. I believe the family was Scotch or Irish, or both, but I do not know."
    See also Judge White's paper in the *Pennsylvania Historical Magazine.*
*Fox, John.
    English; Judge Yerkes, of Bucks.
*Franklin, Walter.
    English Quaker; Samuel Evans.
Franks, Samuel W.
Frazer, Robert S.,
    Answers, "Yes."
*Furst, Austin O.
Futhey, William.
    Judge Hemphill.
Galbraith, John.
    James Sill.
Galbraith, William A.
    James Sill.
Gamble, James.
    C. Larue Munson.
Geyer, John.

Gibson, John (York).
Scotch-Irish on the paternal side; Judge Latimer.

Gilmore, Samuel A.
Judge Crawford, of Greene, and Judge Reppert, of Fayette.

Gordon, Cyrus,
Writes: "Yes; on account of both parents. My father was born in this county (Clearfield) in 1799, a very few years after the family came from Ireland. My information is that his father, Robert Gordon, was Scotch, either he or his parents having emigrated from Scotland to the North of Ireland. His mother, Robert Gordon's wife, Elizabeth Leslie, was Irish, with family home at Armagh, Ireland."

Gordon, David F.
Judge Endlich.

Gordon, James Gay.
Member of Pennsylvania Scotch-Irish Society.

*Green, D. B.

Greenbank, Thomas.

Greer, John M.,
Answers, "Yes."

Grier, Robert C.
See Judge White's paper.

*Gunnison, Frank,
Writes: "I have not the honor of tracing my ancestry back to the Scotch-Irish. My father's ancestors were from Sweden and England, and my mother's came from England."

*Gunster, Frederick W.,
Answers, "No."

*Hagenman, Jeremiah.
German; Judge Endlich.

*Haines, Townsend.
English; Judge Hemphill.

Hale, James T.

Hall, William Maclay.
Answers "Yes" to Judge Longenecker.

*Hallowell, John.

Hamilton, James.

*Hampton, Moses.
English and Welsh; Judge Collier, of Allegheny. See also Judge White's paper.

*Handley, John.
Irish; Judge Archbald.

Hanna, William B.
Member Pennsylvania Scotch-Irish Society.

*Harding, Garrick M.
See Kulp's "Families of the Wyoming Valley."

Hare, J. I. Clark.

Hart, George S.
"His father and mother were both Scotch-Irish"; Judge McIlvaine.

Hawkins, W. G.,
Answers, "Yes."

Hayes, Alexander M.
Samuel Evans.

Hazen, Aaron L.,
Writes: "I am of Scotch-Irish descent. My paternal grandfather, James Warnock, was born at Newtonards, County Down, Ireland, in 1773; came with his parents to America the latter part of the last century, and settled, first at New Castle, Del., and later in Washington county, Pa., and later north of the Ohio river, now Lawrence county, Pennsylvania. My maternal grandmother was of Scotch descent, a daughter of Robert Garton and Betty Lyle, his wife. Robert Lyle, father of Betty, was born in Scotland and came to America in 1742. He was one of the early settlers in Northampton county, Pennsylvania, and on the first grand jury called in said county. The Gartons were Scotch also. My paternal emigrant ancestor was from England—Edward Hazen by name. He was a resident and landowner in Rowley, Mass., in 1649. The Hazen family came to Pennsylvania from Connecticut in 1767, and settled in the Wyoming valley, then Westmoreland, Conn., but departed in 1778, upon the visit to that valley of General Butler, of the king's army, accompanied with his Indian allies. There is also Scotch-Irish blood on my father's side. I have the family record on both sides, in manuscript, quite full from their arrival on American soil."

*Hegins, C. W.
"As far as I can learn, I say no"; Judge Bechtel.

Hemphill, Joseph.
Answers, "Yes."

Henderson, John J.
Judge Thomas, of Crawford.

Henderson, Robert M.
Member Pennsylvania Scotch-Irish Society.

Henry, John Joseph.

Hepburn, Hopewell.
See Judge White's paper.

Hepburn, Samuel.
Judge E. W. Biddle.

*Herman, Martin C.
Judge E. W. Biddle.

*Herrick, Edward.
English; Rodney A. Mercur.

Heston, Edward W.

Heston, Jacob Franklin.

*Hice, Henry.
German; Judge J. S. Wilson, of Beaver. "The name was originally spelled Heis or Heiz."

Hinckley, Henry M.,
　　Writes: "I have always understood that on my mother's side—the Graydons—there was Scotch-Irish blood. Her grandfather came from Ireland. * * * On my father's side—the Hinckleys—the blood is Puritan, coming down directly from Elder Brewster, of the 'Mayflower.'"

Howell, Isaac.

Hoy, Adam.

Hunter, James A.
　　Judges Doty and McConnell, of Westmoreland.

*Ikeler, Elijah R.,
　　Writes: "I possess no Scotch-Irish blood, yet I feel fairly proud of the pure German blood in my veins. The name Ikeler was originally Eggler when my forefathers settled in Massachusetts, where the Yankees converted or perverted it into Ikeler, giving it the sharp Yankee twang."

*Ingersoll, Jared.

Ingham, T. J.

Inghram, James,
　　Writes: "I am about three-fourths Scotch-Irish."

Ingraham, Edward Duffield.

Inskeep, John.

Irvine, William N.

Jackson, David.

Jenkins, Theodore F.

Jenks, W. P.
　　Judge Reed, of Jefferson.

*Jessup, William.

*Jessup, William H.
　　These are father and son. The latter writes: "So far as my father's paternal ancestors are concerned, they trace back to John Jessop, who came from England to Massachusetts, and then to Stamford, Conn., about 1630, and was of English descent, so far as we know. As to my mother's family, they were Harrises, and I have no knowledge of her ancestry back of a few generations, and do not know that they were Scotch-Irish."

Johnston, Robert L.
　　Judge Barker, of Cambria, writes: "Judge Johnston's father came from County Fermanagh, Ireland. His mother, Jane Ramsey, was of Scotch descent. She was born in Huntingdon county, January 7th, 1775."

Johnston, S. P.
　　Judge Noyes and James Sill.

Jones, Joel.

*Jones, J. Pringle.
　　English; Judge Endlich.

Jones, John Richter.

Jordan, Alexander.
　　Judge Savidge, of Northumberland.

Junkin, Benjamin F.

Keen, Reynold.

Kelley, William D.

Kennedy, J. M.,
>Answers, " Yes."

Kidder, Luther.

*Kimmel, F. M.
>German; so stated by his brother, John O. Kimmel, to Judge Longenecker.

King, Alexander.
>Judges John Stewart, of Franklin, and Longenecker; the latter saying: "Judge King's father was of Scotch-Irish extraction, and his mother German, her name being Bergstresser."

King, Edward.

Kirkpatrick, John M.
>Judges Kennedy and William D. Porter.

Kirkpatrick, William S.,
>Writes: "I am proud to be able to say that I am of Scotch-Irish descent on my father's side, as you had a right to infer from the name. My ancestors on the paternal side came to this country from the North of Ireland before the Revolution, settling near Basking Ridge, Somerset county, New Jersey."

*Knapp, Henry M.
>New York; Judge Archbald.

Knight, Jonathan T.

Knox, James B.
>Judge Reed.

*Koch, Richard,
>Writes: "My ancestors were German."

*Krause, David.
>German; Judge Swartz. Judge Yerkes writes: "He was born in Lebanon, Lebanon county, November 2d, 1800, and was the son of David and Regina Krause."

*Krebs, David L.

*Landis, A. L.

Latimer, James W.
>Member Pennsylvania Scotch-Irish Society.

Lindsey, James.
>Judges Crawford and Reppert. Judge McIlvaine writes: "James Lindsey was the son of John Lindsey, a Scotchman, and Mary Hughes Lindsey, the daughter of an Irishman."

Linn, Samuel.
>Judge Love.

Livingston, John B.,
>Writes: "My grandfather on my father's side was English; my grandfather on my mother's side was Scotch-Irish."

Logan, James A.
>Member Pennsylvania Scotch-Irish Society.

*Long, Henry G.
   German; Samuel Evans.
*Longaker, A. B.,
   Writes: "I am paternal Swiss and maternal Dutch."
*Longenecker, J. H.,
   Writes: "My own ancestors were Swiss and German."
Love, John G.,
   Writes as follows: "My grandfather, Robert Love, came from the northern part of Ireland; I don't know exact locality. His parents died en voyage, or shortly after arriving in this country, when he was a child of about seven years. He arrived in 1785. He learned the printing trade in Lancaster. In the year 1800 he married a Quaker lady of Lancaster, Miss Lydia Jane Hart. Shortly afterwards he moved to Philadelphia, where my father, James Love, was born. He attended public schools in Philadelphia and was one of the school children that took part in the welcome to Lafayette on his return to America about 1821. My grandfather was of Scotch-Irish descent, and Presbyterian in religious faith. My father came to Warrior's Mark, Huntingdon county, in 1833; carried on merchant tailoring there for about three years, then moved to Stormstown, Centre county, where he carried on the same business. In 1839 was married to Miss Catharine Gray. I was born in Stormstown, Centre county, December 10th, 1843. I presume I am of Scotch-Irish descent."

Ludlow, James R.
   Judge Audenried.
Lynch, John.
Lynd, James.
Lyon, T. H. B.
Lyons, Jeremiah.
Magee, Christopher.
   Judges Kennedy and W. D. Porter.
*Mallory, Garrick.
   English; Judge Endlich.
Maxwell, Henry D.
   Judge Schuyler, of Northampton,
Maxwell, William.
   Judges Schuyler and Scott.
*Mayer, Charles A.,
   Answers, "No."
*Maynard, John W.
   New England; C. Larue Munson. See also Judge White's paper.
McCalmont, Alexander.
   Judges Olmsted, of Potter; Morrison, of McKean; and Reed, of Jefferson.
McCalmont, John S.
McCartney, Washington.
   Judges Schuyler and Scott.
McClean, William.
   Judge Swope, of Adams.

McClung, Samuel A.,
  Writes: "I am to a considerable degree Scotch-Irish. My mother's grandfather came from the North of Ireland and settled in Western Pennsylvania at the close of the Revolutionary War, and my ancestors on that side have since lived in Westmoreland and Allegheny counties. My father's father came from Scotland to New York city, where my father was born in 1808. In 1836 my father moved to Allegheny county from Philadelphia, and spent the remainder of his life here."

McClure, Harold M.,
  Answers, "Yes."

McClure, William B.
  Judges Hawkins, Kennedy, W. D. Porter, and J. W. F. White.

McConnell, Alex. D.,
  Answers, "Yes."

McDermitt, Arcus.
  Judge Miller, of Mercer.

*MacEnally, J. B.
  Irish and German; Judge Gordon, of Clearfield.

McGuffin, Lawrence.

McIlvaine, John A.,
  Answers, "Yes."

McJunkin, Ebenezer.

McKean, Joseph Borden.

McMichael, Charles B.
  Judge Audenried.

McMichael, John.

McMullen, David.

McPherson, John B.
  Member Pennsylvania Scotch-Irish Society.

*Meily, Frank E.,
  Writes: "My ancestors on both sides are of German origin."

Mehard, Samuel S.

Mellon, Thomas.
  Member Pennsylvania Scotch-Irish Society.

*Mestrezat, S. L.,
  Writes: "I am of French descent."

*Metzger, John J.,
  Answers, "No." C. Larue Munson writes that he was born in Allentown and his parents in Germany.

*Meyers, Oliver H.

Miller, Samuel H.,
  Answers, "Yes."

Mitchell, John I.,
  Writes: "The father of my grandmother Mitchell was born in Scotland, Thomas Kenny, Sr., of Hartford, Conn., and he was in the patriot army in the revolutionary war. My grandfather Mitchell was of Scotch-Irish descent, and was born in Orange county, New Jersey."

*Moore, Jesse.
> English; James Sill.

Moore, John.
> Judges Doty and McConnell.

Moore, Thomas L.

Morgan, Benjamin R.

Morgan, George W.

Morrison, Thomas A.,
> Answers, "Yes."

*Morrow, P. D.
> Irish; Rodney A. Mercur.

Morton, George.

Moulder, William.

Neale, James B.,
> Writes: "James B. Neale, son of the late Dr. Samuel S. Neale, of New Jersey colonial ancestry, and Margaret Brown Neale, born in city of Pittsburgh, Pa., 27th February, 1837. A direct descendant, on the mother's side, of James Brown, a Scotchman, and a soldier in the famous Enniskillen Dragoons, comprised entirely of men six feet two without a shoe. Killed at the battle of the Boyne.
> "The grandfather, Robert Brown, a true type of the Scotch-Irish, was born in Ireland, county of Fermanagh, in 1775; came to this country in 1795, and in 1796 was married in the Presbyterian Church of Carlisle, Pa., to Rebecca, daughter of James Brown, a veteran of the Revolution. About 1798 he removed to Indiana county, and shortly afterward to Armstrong county, to the present site of Kittanning, of which he was one of the founders and largest property owners. During life he was a prominent citizen. At the beginning of the century he was appointed one of the first justices in commission in the county. Died in 1858. Margaret Brown, his third child, was born in 1803, in Kittanning, and died in 1851.
> "James B. Neale acquired the elements of his education in the common school of Kittanning, but in his fourteenth year began his business career in Kittanning, in 1851, ending with a prominent position as business manager of the manufacturing house of Brown, Floyd & Co., in Pittsburgh, in 1858. Immediately thereafter he entered the law office of Golden & Fulton, in Kittanning, from which, on motion of Hon. Samuel A. Purviance, he was admitted to the bar at March Term, 1862, but before his admission attending the Elder's Ridge Academy for one year. Soon after his admission he entered into partnership with Edward S. Golden. After the termination of the partnership in 1871, he went to Europe and entered the University of Leipzig. On his return he resumed the practice of law, engaging also in the production of oil, as well as editing the *Union Free Press*, of Kittanning. In 1879, on the death of Judge Boggs, he was appointed by Governor Hoyt president judge of the thirty-third district, to which he was elected in the same year, filling the position until the 1st of January, 1890. At the close of his political term, associated with J. H. Painter, Esq., he resumed the practice of law, in which he is still engaged. In July, 1897, he accepted the presidency of the Merchants' national bank of Kittanning. In 1885 he was married to Annie E., daughter of the late Simon Truby, Jr.

Nill, James.
    Judges John Stewart and Rowe.
*Noyes, Charles H.,
    Writes: "For my own part, I am pretty near the pure-blooded Yankee. There is a tinge of Scotch, but no Scotch-Irish blood. I suppose that accounts for my indifferent success in life."
O'Brien, Dennis W.
Ogle, Charles.
Olmsted, Arthur G.,
    Answers, "Yes."
*Orvis, John H.
Over, J. W.,
    Answers, "Yes; on the maternal side."
Parry, Edward Owen.
*Parsons, Anson V.
Patterson, David W.
    (Judge Patterson was the father of my wife, and I know that his ancestry was Scotch-Irish.—J. B. McP.)
Patton, Benjamin, Jr.
    Judges Kennedy and W. D. Porter. See also Judge White's paper.
*Pearson, John J.
    English; on the authority of his daughters, residing in Harrisburg.
*Peck, Benjamin M.
    New England; Rodney A. Mercur.
Peckham, Aaron K.
Pierce, William S.
    Judge Audenried.
Pennypacker, Samuel W.,
    Writes: "My father was Isaac Anderson Pennypacker, a physician, whose mother, Sarah Anderson, was a daughter of the Hon. Isaac Anderson, lieutenant in the Revolution, presidential elector for James Madison, and member of Congress from 1803 to 1807, and was a son of Major Patrick Anderson, who commanded the Pennsylvania Musketry Battalion in the Revolutionary War. His father was James Anderson, who came here direct from the Isle of Skye. I am also a descendant of the Antrims of New Jersey, who, I believe, came from the North of Ireland."
Penrose, Clement B.,
    Writes: "My mother's paternal grandfather was Capt. William McFeen, of the British Navy, and while I have to confess to a want of knowledge on the subject, though I could, perhaps, be informed by some of my relatives, I infer from the 'Mc' that he was of Scotch or Irish descent. All of my other ancestors, so far as I know—Penrose on the one side and Biddle on the other—were, I think, English or Welsh, although I find in Foss's 'The Judges of England,' mention made of John Penros, of a Cornish family, who was raised to the office of Judge of the King's Bench, in Ireland, on February 27th, 1385: 8 Richard II., Col. Rot. Pat., 211."
*Pershing, Cyrus L.
    Writes that he is German.

Pettis, S. N.
Pettit, Thomas McKean.
*Pickering, Timothy.
Pollock, James.
    Judge Savidge.
Porter, James M.
Porter, Robert.
    Judge William W. Porter, of the Superior Court, writes: "James Madison Porter was born on June 6th, 1793; admitted to the bar on April 24th, 1813; settled in Easton in 1818; practiced law for forty years; a member of the Constitutional Convention of 1838; defeated for president of that body by John Sergeant by one vote; subsequently presided over the convention during Mr. Sergeant's absence as a member of Congress. He became president judge of the district composed of the counties of Dauphin, Lebanon, and Schuylkill, and while holding that office was appointed by President Tyler Secretary of War. On retiring from this position he resumed the practice of his profession, and was afterwards elected judge of the district which then lay at the extreme northeastern portion of the state. He resigned this office from ill health, and died at his home in Easton on the 11th of November, 1862.

"I find a reference in the same article to Robert Porter, who was a half brother of James M. Porter, being the son of Gen. Andrew Porter by his first wife. Robert was born January 10th, 1768; served during the Revolution as lieutenant; was admitted to the bar on May 15th, 1789; and practiced law in Philadelphia. He was appointed by Governor Snyder judge of the third judicial district, composed of the counties of Berks, Lehigh, and Northampton. He discharged the duties of this office for many years, and then resigned his commission and retired to private life. He died in Brookville, Pa., on the 23d of June, 1842."

Potts, James.
    Judge Barker.
Pratt, Joseph T.
*Purdy, George S.
Randall, Archibald.
Rayburn, Calvin,
    Writes: "As to myself, I am of Scotch-Irish ancestry on my mother's side of the house, and Scotch on my father's. On my mother's side my grandmother was born in Ireland, and on my father's side my great grandfather was born in Scotland."
Redman, Joseph.
Reed, Henry.
Reed, John W.,
    Answers, "Yes."
*Reppert, Edmund H.,
    Writes: "I am very much mixed—mostly German, with a dash of Welsh, Irish, and Scotch, a little of old Adam mellowed by age, &c. It is possible that my maternal grandmother was Scotch-Irish."
Riddle, James.
    Dr. Egle, J. Simpson Africa, of Huntingdon, and Judge Longenecker.

Ritchie, David.
    Judges Kennedy and W. D. Porter. See also Judge White's paper.

Roberts, Samuel.
    Judge McIlvaine writes: "Samuel Roberts was born in Philadelphia. His ancestor came to Pennsylvania with the first emigrants. His grandfather was sheriff of Philadelphia county from 1716 to 1721. Judge Roberts was the author of 'Roberts' Digest of British Statutes in Force in Pennsylvania.' I could not find from what county the Robertses emigrated."

*Rhone, D. L.

Robinson, William, Jr.

*Rockefeller, William M.
    Dutch and English; Judge Savidge.

Ross, John.

Ross, Henry P.
    These are grandfather and grandson. A newspaper article by Judge Yerkes, too long to publish here, is deposited with the Society and contains a great deal of information about the family.

Rowe, David Watson,
    Writes: "I am of Scotch-Irish ancestry. On my father's side the Rowes were English, and settled in Ireland in the English pale, County Westmeath. The Wises were Scotch-Irish. On my mother's side the Watsons were Scotch-Irish; the Prathers, English. So that I appear to be half English and half Scotch-Irish.
    "The Wises and Prathers settled in this country at a very early day. The Watsons came from Lancaster county, where they were before the Revolutionary war, and Col. James Watson was a colonel of the Second Battalion, Lancaster county, in the time of the Revolution. My grandfather Rowe came from Ireland in 1804, and was a private in the War of 1812."

Ryon, James.
    On the authority of his brother; reported by Judge Bechtel.

Sadler, Wilbur F.
    Judge E. W. Biddle.

*Sassaman, A. H.
    German; Judge Endlich.

*Savidge, Clinton R.
    Writes that he is of Dutch and English ancestry.

*Schuyler, William W.,
    Answers, "No."

Scofield, Glenni W.
    Judge Reed.

Scott, David.
    George B. Kulp, of Wilkesbarre, writes: "An ancestor of Judge Scott was at the battle of Culloden or Drumossie Moor, near Inverness, Scotland, which was fought April 16th, 1776. After the defeat of the Scottish troops, Judge Scott's ancestor went to the county of Cavan, Ireland, and subsequently one of his sons emigrated to the Berkshire Hills, Massachusetts, and the other to Virginia. Gen. Winfield S. Scott was a decendant of the Virginia branch, and Judge Scott of the Massachusetts family."

Scott, Henry W.,
Writes: "My grandfather emigrated from Donegal, a county of Ulster, in the North of Ireland, about 1810. My mother was born here, but has been long dead. My father is not living either. My grandfather's name was Oliver Erwin, and he was a Presbyterian. He died in 1853 in Bucks county."

*Searle, D. W.,
Answers, "No."

Seeley, Henry M.

Shafer, John D.
Judges Frazer, Kennedy, and W. D. Porter.

*Shaler, Charles.
Irish descent; Judge Hawkins of Allegheny. Judge W. D. Porter says he was not Scotch-Irish, and Judge White thinks he was of New England ancestry.

*Shannon, Peter C.
Irish. See Judge White's paper.

*Sharswood, James.

*Shippen, Henry.
James Sill writes: "Henry Shippen was from Huntingdon county, which county he represented in the Assembly in 1823-24. He was of stalwart form, and a terror to evildoers. You know he convicted and sentenced Francisco in 1837. From my recollection of the judge and knowledge of his characteristics and of the settlers in the Juniata Valley, I believe him to have been Scotch-Irish."

Samuel Evans, however, gives a more accurate account: "Hon. Henry Shippen was the son of Hon. Joseph Shippen, who was the son of Edward Shippen, prothonotary of Lancaster. Henry Shippen studied law in Lancaster with James Hopkins, Esq., and was admitted to the bar in 1811. About 1815 he married my second cousin, Elizabeth Evans, daughter of Evan Evans, Esq., a prominent lawyer of Sunbury, Pa., who died in 1811. Henry and Elizabeth Shippen were married at grandmother Evans, who then resided on the south side of West King street, Lancaster, second door east of Prince street. Mr. Shippen moved to Huntingdon, and practiced law there a few years, and was appointed judge of that district by Governor Schultz, and afterwards transferred to Crawford county district. He was a handsome man, with fine military carriage. He commanded a company of mounted volunteers in the War of 1812. My uncle, Jasper Slaymaker, and President Buchanan, also were with them to Cecil County, Maryland, and Baltimore. The Shippens were English Quakers; afterwards belonged to the English Church. Henry Shippen left a large family, all of whom became Unitarians, and are prominent people. * * * Henry Shippen's mother was a lady of English descent."

Simmons, Anthony.

Simonton, John W.
Member Pennsylvania Scotch-Irish Society.

*Sittser, John A.,
Answers, "No."

Slagle, Jacob F.,
Writes: "My father was of German descent. The name was originally spelled Schlegel. His mother was also German. My mother was of Scotch descent. Her maiden name was Allison."

Smith, Charles.

Smith, Jonathan Bayard.
   Judge Arnold.

*Smyser, Daniel M.
   His son, E. M. Smyser, of Philadelphia, writes: "My father was of German descent on both sides." Judge Yerkes says: "Daniel M. Smyser was from Gettysburg. The late Judge Wills was his son in law."

Sommer, Jacob.

*Souther, Henry.
   James Sill writes: "His parents were both of English extraction. Judge Souther was a native of Charlestown, Mass. He came to that part of Elk county which was embraced before in Jefferson county in 1842. He afterwards studied law and was admitted in   to the bar of Elk county. In 1855 he was elected from the district of Tioga, Potter, Elk, Jefferson, Forest, and Clearfield to the Senate. In 1871 he was appointed judge, and removed in 1872, after his judicial service, to Erie county. He died in 1894 or 1895."

*Spayd, John.
   German; Judge Endlich.

Stanton, W. H.

Stewart, John.
   Member Pennsylvania Scotch-Irish Society.

Stewart, W. F. Bay,
   Writes: "I may say I am almost entirely of Scotch-Irish extraction—thirty-one out of thirty-two parts."

Stinson, H.,
   Answers, "Yes."

*Storm, John B.,
   Writes: "All my ancestors, paternal and maternal, were German."

Stowe, Edwin H.
   Judges Kennedy and W. D. Porter.

*Streeter, Ferris B.
   Dutch; Rodney A. Mercur.

Stroud, George M.

*Sulzberger, Mayer,
   Answers, "No."

Sutherland, Joel B.

*Swartz, Aaron S.,
   Answers, "No."

*Swartz, H. H.,
   German; Judge Endlich.

Swope, S. McC.,
   Answers, "Yes."

Taylor, Charles E.

Taylor, George.
   Judges Barker, of Cambria, and Martin Bell, of Blair, and J. Simpson Africa.

*Taylor, Henry.

*Taylor, James F.
>These are great grandfather and great grandson. Judge McIlvaine writes that Henry Taylor, the first judge commissioned after the organization of Washington county, was of Irish descent. His great grandson adds that he was twice appointed—once October 2d, 1781, and again on September 30th, 1788. On the 19th of April, 1783, during the Wayne expedition against the Indians, he was commissioned by Governor Mifflin brigadier-general of the brigade composed of the militia of Washington county. He came from Cecil county, Maryland, in 1770.

Thayer, M. Russell.

Thomas, Frank J.,
>Answers, "Yes; in a marked degree."

Thompson, Alexander.
>Judges Longenecker and John Stewart.

Thompson, Oswald.
>Judge Audenried.

*Van Reed, H.
>German; Judge Endlich.

Vaux, Roberts.

Vincent, J. P.
>James Sill writes: "Judge Vincent's name is French, but through his mother he is of Scotch descent."

Waddell, W. B.
>Judge Hemphill.

Wallace, William D.,
>Writes: "My father was Scotch-Irish, and my mother a full-bred Scotch woman."

Waller, C. P.

*Walling, Emory A.,
>Writes: "I was born in Erie county, but am of New England ancestry."

Walker, Jonathan.
>Dr. Egle and J. Simpson Africa.

Walker, Thomas H.
>Lewis B. Walker, his son, writes as follows: "Thomas H. Walker, born 1822, was the son of Lewis and Sarah Yeates (Hubley) Walker.
>"Sarah Y. Hubley, born December 22d, 1789, was the daughter of Jacob and Margaret (Burd) Hubley.
>"Margaret Burd, born July 3d, 1761, was the daughter of Col. James Burd and his wife, Sarah, daughter of Edward Shippen, of Lancaster.
>"Col. James Burd was born in Scotland, March 10th, 1725. He was the son of Edward Burd (born February 18th, 1700) and his wife, Jean Haliburton. Col. James Burd emigrated to America about 1746. He was a colonel in the Pennsylvania service in the war 1755-64. Various letters of Colonel Burd are published in the Colonial Records and Pennsylvania Archives, first series.
>"His journal kept in February, 1758, is published in Third Pennsylvania Archives, first series, page 352. In vols. II. and VII. of

second series of Pennsylvania Archives other journals of Colonel Burd are published. The sketch in the Commemorative and Biographical Encyclopedia of Dauphin County, page 173, is not entirely correct. Colonel Burd built Tinian, still standing at Highspire, six miles from Harrisburg. Colonel Burd's daughter Sarah was married to Jasper Yeates, judge, &c. His son, Edward Burd, was for a long period Prothonotary of the Supreme Court.

"(NOTE.—The writer is preparing for publication a large quantity of material to be called 'The Burd Papers.' One volume has been already issued, and has the additional title, 'Extracts from Chief Justice William Allen's Letter Book.' A copy is in the State Library.)"

Watson, James.
Judge Crawford.

*Watson, Richard.
English; Judge Yerkes.

Watts, Frederick.
Judge E. W. Biddle.

*Weand, H. G.,
Answers "No."

Weidman, Mason.
Grant Weidman, Jr., of Lebanon, writes: "I am informed that my uncle Mason's grandfather, William Murray, was born in Ireland in 1792, and came to America when he was five years old."

*Wetmore, L. D.
Long Island; James Sill.

White, Thomas.

White, Harry.
These are father and son. Judge Harry White writes as follows: "About Thomas White, the second judge of the old 10th, my revered father, I presume to inclose you a sketch. His ancestry you can gather from it.

"I am one of those peculiarly American people who believe every tub should stand on its own bottom, to use a trite phrase. That is, not to rely on the prestige of ancestry for success; hence I have not been vigilant in looking up my pedigree, although my daughter has.

"You will observe, if you look at the sketch of father, that on his side the blood of the Perrys got into my circulation. Commodore Oliver Hazard Perry, of Perry's 'Victory' fame, was among my kindred, and my grandfather, Richard White, is buried, in Christ Church graveyard, Philadelphia. My mother's name, born in Huntingdon county, was McConnell. Her father was Alexander McConnell, after whom McConnellstown is called. I never saw him, but his house was the headquarters of the old Seceder, now the United Presbyterian church, in this section. Of course, he was a sturdy old Scotch-Irishman. My grandmother, his wife, was Judith Floyd in her maiden day. She was born near Leesburg, Va., as I have it. Of course, as her name indicates, on her father's side she was Welsh. On her mother's side I have always understood she was Scotch-Irish, as the phrase goes. The wife of your townsman, A. J. Dull, Esq., who was a couple of classes ahead of me at Princeton, is called after my grandmother. She was the great friend of the late Governor Porter, who lived in Huntingdon and came to his assistance in some of his early financial annoyances. She was a remarkable woman, and died here at my father's house ninety-three years of age. I dwell on her memory because I was about the youngest of her descendants, and her love and tenderness hallow to me her memory. Of my other predecessors I shall not speak, as you say you have their pedigree. You will find some reference of them, or some of them, in the sketch of Thomas White I inclose."

White, Robert G.

White, John W. F.
See his paper in the *Pennsylvania Historical Magazine.*

*Wickes, Pere L.
Judge Bittinger writes: " He was a Marylander from the Eastern shore, and, I think, of English descent."

Williams, Jonathan.

Williamson, W. McK.
Judge Bailey.

*Williston, Horace.
English; Judge Olmsted.

Wills, David.
Was member Pennsylvania Scotch-Irish Society.

Willson, Alpheus E.
Judges Crawford and Reppert, and J. Simpson Africa.

Willson, Robert M.
Judge Audenried.

Wilkins, William.

Wilmot, David.

Wilson, Abraham S.
John Blair Linn, of Bellefonte.

Wilson, Bird.
Judge Yerkes has written a very full sketch of Judge Wilson, which is filed among the Society's papers.

Wilson, James Sharp.
Judge Wilson sends the following sketch :—
" I am Scotch-Irish.
"1. Thomas Wilson was an officer in King William's army, among the first to cross the river Boyne on horseback on the morning of July 1st, 1690. He was rewarded for his bravery with a grant of land. He resided in County Cavan, Ireland, having an extensive bleach-green within a mile of Coote Hill. His ancestors had emigrated from Scotland to Ireland. He had but one son.
"2. Hugh Wilson, born 1689, in County Cavan, Ireland, married Sarah Craig in Ireland, emigrated to America, and settled in 'The Irish Settlement,' Northampton county, Pennsylvania, as early as 1736. His home lay northwest of what is now known as Howerton, in Allen township. Upon the erection of that county in 1752, he was one of the commissioners named in the Act to purchase land at Easton for court house and prison, and on June 9th, 1752, was commissioned one of the justices, and as such assisted to hold the first courts in Northampton county. He died in 1773, and is buried in the old graveyard at the settlement. He had several children, direct line.

" 3. Thomas Wilson, born in 1724, married Elizabeth Hayes in 1760. He removed from 'The Irish Settlement' in 1792 to the Buffalo valley, now Union county. He died February 25th, 1799, aged seventy-four years, according to the inscription on his tombstone in Lewisburg cemetery. His widow removed to Beaver county in 1808 with her sons, William and Thomas.

" 4. Thomas Wilson, born June 17th, 1775, married Agnes Hemphill October 7th, 1806 (a sister of Judge Hemphill). He died July 7th, 1860, leaving eleven children to survive him.

" 5. John H. Wilson, born May 22d, 1822, married Mary Elizabeth Mehard March 8th, 1849. He was an ambitious, energetic man, extensively engaged in farming. Was elected county commissioner on the Republican ticket in 1890, and died in the midst of his term. He left six children to survive him.

" 6. James Sharp Wilson."

Wilson, Stephen F.
Judge Morrison, of McKean.

Wilson, Theophilus S.
Judge Reed.

Wiltbank, William W.,
Writes: "My mother was Elizabeth White Macpherson, the daughter of Gen. William Macpherson, who was the son of John Macpherson, who came to this country in 1745. John Macpherson had been a writer to the Signet in Edinburgh, and he left Scotland because of the reverses of that year, having been an adherent of Cluny Macpherson, who was his first cousin."

Wolbert, Frederick.

Woods, George.
Judge Longenecker.

Woods, S. S.
Judge Bailey, of Huntingdon, and John Blair Linn.

*Woodward, Stanley,
Answers, "No."

Yerkes, Harman.

Yerkes, William H.
Judge Harman Yerkes, of Bucks, writes: "My father's mother, Mary Long, was the daughter of Capt. Andrew Long, of the Continental army, who was appointed associate judge here in 1788. Her father was a Scotch-Irishman. The late Judge William Harman Yerkes, of Philadelphia, was also a grandson of Capt. Andrew Long."

Young, John.
Was born in Glasgow, July 12th, 1762, and came directly to Pennsylvania; Judges Doty, McConnell, Rayburn, and Harry White.

APPENDIX C.

PHILADELPHIA, PA., February 1st, 1898.

To the Members of the Pennsylvania Scotch-Irish Society:

GENTLEMEN:—A copy of the report of the proceedings of your Society at their eighth annual meeting and banquet, held in Philadelphia, February 27th, 1897, has just been sent to me. I notice in it a speech by Judge Stewart, in which he says that I have grossly defamed the Scotch-Irish, and he assails with the greatest violence, with "indignation and resentment," as he puts it, a book of mine, "Pennsylvania: Colony and Commonwealth," which was published a year or so ago.

I heard of the Judge's speech soon after it was delivered. Some friends of mine spoke to me of it as a joke, and I supposed it had been merely ordinary criticism or difference of opinion, and, as I did not know of its being published, gave myself no further thought about it. I never became aware of its full enormity and absurdity until I read it a few days ago. I am told that it was still worse as delivered, and has been toned down to go in print. But the toning did not go far enough. Unless I say something about it I shall be in the position of allowing the Judge to falsify Pennsylvania history; for his wild statements now stand approved by the whole Scotch-Irish Society, and are given out to the world as history in one of their regular publications.

I do not care to parade the matter in the newspapers because, so far as I know, Judge Stewart's speech was not in the newspapers. It was delivered to a private society, and is now printed in their regular proceedings. I therefore mail a copy of this letter to every member of the Society whose address is given in the report which I have.

The Judge seems to be a survival of those old-time cutting and slashing orators we read about; and his knowledge of history is, as might be expected, highly imaginative. Of course, I know that he labored under several serious disadvantages. The dinner and its accompaniments had been in progress for some time before he began. He was almost the last speaker, and he tells us in the beginning of his speech that he is brought in at the dregs. Under such circumstances a man is tempted to do something extravagant to arouse the jaded attention, and the best way is to assume that the dearest interests of his hearers are attacked or defamed, and then pose as defending them. This is a good after-dinner device, but it is not good for the truth of history.

He charges in the most extravagant and unjudicial language that I am a "perverter of the truth" of history and the author of "a studied and deliberate libel," and, as an instance, says that I have without foundation or authority accused the Scotch-Irish of cowardice when Colonel Bouquet was setting out from Carlisle in 1763 to save Fort Pitt, which had been taken by Pontiac.

"With equal recklessness of statement, and in a like spirit of unfairness, he charges that in 1763, when Bouquet passed through the valley on his way to the Ohio and beyond to suppress the conspiracy of Pontiac, this people were too indifferent or cowardly to recruit his ranks, and too mean to supply him with transportation."

* * * * * *

"I challenge Mr. Fisher again for his proofs that anybody but himself has ever made such complaint."

Now, what I actually did say after describing how Bouquet arrived at Carlisle with the remains of two invalid regiments from the West Indies, was as follows:—

"Not a man of the Scotch-Irish frontiersmen joined him. They were slow at furnishing him with wagons and caused him many delays. They were indeed broken and demoralized, and stayed at home, they said, to protect their families; and, moreover, they believed that the Colonel and his sick list were doomed. ('Pennsylvania: Colony and Commonwealth,' 225.)"

In the above passage I charge no one with cowardice. I do not say that they were too mean to furnish transportation; I say they were slow about it, and I give reasons for all their conduct which would satisfy any one in a reasonable frame of mind. I wrote the passage as it stands, not because I am a Quaker, as the Judge says; I am not a Quaker and never was one; nor because I hate the Scotch-Irish or am prejudiced against them; nor for any of the other silly motives which were assigned at the banquet; but because the authorities, Bouquet's letters, and the writings of men who lived at the time support such a statement and compel you to write it without regard to what your feelings may be.

Provost Smith, of the College of Philadelphia, lived at that time and was an earnest promoter of all warlike operations against the French and Indians. Judge Stewart says he was a Scotch-Irishman; but that is simply another of the Judge's blunders. The Provost wrote, however, a history of Bouquet's expedition which he knew all about, and I will quote what he says on this point:—

"Early orders had been given to prepare a convoy of provisions on the frontiers of Pennsylvania, but such were the universal terror and consternation of the inhabitants that when Colonel Bouquet arrived at Carlisle nothing had yet been done.

"In the midst of that general confusion, the supplies necessary for the expedition became very precarious, nor was it less difficult to procure horses and carriages for the use of the troops.

* * * * * * *

"Their march did not abate the fears of the dejected inhabitants. They knew the strength and ferocity of the enemy. They remembered the former defeats even of our best troops, and were full of diffidence and apprehensions on beholding the small number and sickly state of the regulars employed in this expedition. Without the least hopes, therefore, of success, they seemed only to wait for the fatal event, which they dreaded, to abandon all the country beyond the Susquehanna.

"In such despondency of mind, it is not surprising that though their whole was at stake, and depended entirely upon the fate of this little army, none of them offered to assist in the defense of the country by joining the expedition; in which they would have been of infinite service, being, in general, well acquainted with the woods, and excellent marksmen. ('History of Bouquet's Expedition,' pages 10, 11, 12.)"

Parkman, in his "Conspiracy of Pontiac," tells the same story. He used Provost Smith's book as his authority, and had also some manuscript letters of Bouquet, which, possibly, Provost Smith never saw.

"To return to Bouquet, who lay encamped at Carlisle, urging on his preparations, but met by obstacles at every step. Wagons and horses had been promised, but promises were broken, and all was vexation and delay. The Province of Pennsylvania, from causes to be shown hereafter, would do nothing to aid the troops who were defending it; and even the people from the frontier, partly from the apathy and confusion of terror, and partly, it seems, from dislike and jealousy of the regulars, were backward and sluggish in co-operating with them. 'I hope,' writes Bouquet to Sir Jeffrey Amherst, 'that we shall be able to save that infatuated people from destruction notwithstanding all their endeavors to defeat your vigorous measures. I meet everywhere with the same backwardness, even among the most exposed of the inhabitants, which makes everything move on heavily, and is disgusting to the last degree.' And, again, 'I find myself utterly abandoned by the very people I am ordered to protect.' ('Conspiracy of Pontiac,' vol. II., pages 48, 49.) "

Judge Stewart takes great pains to tell us in his speech that he has studied with much care the history of the Scotch-Irish in Pennsylvania, but he seems to have overlooked the most obvious and ordinary authorities with which a single visit or inquiry at an historical society or library would have supplied him. If he had even taken the trouble to look in "Gordon's History of Pennsylvania" (a dull book but a very accurate one), pages 399 and 400, he would have found the statements made in the above quotations substantially repeated.

I will ask the Judge's conscience and Scotch-Irish integrity to say whether, in view of the above authorities, it was proper for a man in his position, to charge me, as he does in his speech, with "a studied and deliberate libel," or to say that I am "a perverter of the truth" of history, and then afterwards print such assertions.

He goes on to say:—

"Mr. Fisher knows, or ought to know, that Bouquet, a British officer in command of British troops, called for no recruits, and was without any authority to make such a call."

But Parkman says: "He had attempted to engage a body of frontiersmen to join him on the march; but they preferred to remain for the defense of their families" ("Conspiracy of Pontiac," vol. II., page 56); and I leave the Judge and Parkman to fight it out between them.

If the Judge was a real Scotch-Irishman, his sense of humor, which is usually characteristic of that race, would save him from such statements. Bouquet, of course, had no authority to compel the Scotch-Irish to serve. That is the very point. The Scotch-Irish would not go unless they were compelled by force. They would not be volunteers, and the Judge, without knowing it, is making an argument to show that his own people were cowards and would not fight for their own safety.

But I must rescue the Scotch-Irish from such an unskillful defender. They were not cowards. They had reasons for not going with Bouquet, and I have given those reasons in "Pennsylvania: Colony and Commonwealth." No one has ever suggested that they were cowards except the Judge.

In another part of his tirade he says: "The settlers in the Kittochtiny Valley seem to be the special objects of Mr. Fisher's antipathy." That is a pure assumption on the part of the Judge. I cannot find that I mention them specially anywhere in the book, and there was no reason why I should make any special mention of them separate from the rest of the Scotch-Irish of the Province. I have no antipathy to them. On the contrary, I think they were then, and most of them are to-day, among the very best of the Scotch-Irish people.

But the Judge was making a speech at the close of a banquet and had to manufacture it out of nothing, and this assumption about my antipathy was dragged in to bolster up another assumption, that I had in some way accused the Kittochtiny people of murdering Indians and cheating them out of their land. I never accused them of anything of the kind.

"I challenge Mr. Fisher," he says, "to show a murder or an outrage upon an Indian in that valley committed by the hand of a Scotch-Irish settler during all that period from 1730 to 1755. I challenge him to show a single complaint of unjust appropriation of land east of the Tuscarora Mountain in that time."

The first challenge is a very absurd one, because I never said that the settlers of the Kittochtiny Valley committed murder or outrages on Indians in that valley; nor have I said anywhere that any of the Scotch-Irish in any part of the Province committed murders or outrages on Indians between 1730 and 1755. That was a period of peace before the wars began, and there are pages and pages in my book showing that it was a period of peace all over the Province. Such a challenge and such talk are totally irrelevant.

In the second challenge, if the Judge had confined himself to the land east of the Kittochtiny range instead of east of the Tuscarora, I might have said that I knew of none that had been improperly appropriated. I never said there was any, although there may have been, for all I know. But as he has gone farther westward, and said land east of the Tuscarora range, I can say that, while I never made such an assertion in my book, there was, according to authority, some land improperly appropriated close to the Tuscarora range, and on the east side of it, in the Path Valley, as it was called, which lay between the Tuscarora and the Kittochtiny; and this I will show presently.

In "Pennsylvania: Colony and Commonwealth," I have nowhere said that there was any unjust appropriation of land in the Kittochtiny Valley. I do not even raise the question. What I do say, however, is that the Scotch-Irish and German frontiersmen were guilty, in numerous instances, of going upon land and settling there before it had been purchased from the Indians, and this caused a great deal of irritation. If the Judge means to deny this statement, he takes a great deal on himself; for it is vouched for by every one who has the slightest knowledge of our Colonial history.

The principal authority is a book called "The Alienation of the Indians," written by Charles Thomson, who lived in those times, was deeply and actively interested in the Indian question, and thoroughly familiar with it. He was afterwards Secretary of the Continental Congress, and a man very much respected. He was a Scotch-Irishman, it is said, and he reports the Indians as saying, in the treaty of 1742:—

"Your people," say they to the Governor, "daily settle on these lands and spoil our hunting. We must insist on your removing them; as you know, they have no right to settle to the northward of the Kittochtinny Hills. In particular we renew our complaints against some people who are settled at Juniata, a branch of the Susquehanna, and all along the banks of that river as far as Mahaniay. ('Alienation of the Indians,' page 49.)"

In another passage he describes how the intrusion by the frontiersmen on the Indian land in 1750 became so outrageous that it was feared there would be a massacre, unless these intruders were at once removed.

"After this Mr. Peters proceeded, and being accompanied with those Indians, broke up the settlements in Sherman's Valley, on Juniata, at Aucquick (*alias* Aughwick), in the Path Valley and Big Cove, which all lie beyond the Kittochtinny Hills, everywhere dispossessing the people. * * * The people of the little cove which was a part of the unpurchased lands just on the borders of Maryland, presented him a petition, addressed to the Governor, praying that they might be allowed to remain there till the purchase was made of the lands from the Indians. (Page 71.)"

It will be observed that he says that there was unlawful intrusion in the Path Valley, which lay between the Kittochtiny and the Tuscarora Mountains. Many of the places he mentions lay immediately to the westward and northward of the Kittochtiny Valley, and all the places were close to the Scotch-Irish settlements. If the Judge really thinks that the Scotch-Irish never intruded on Indian land, I cannot envy him his credulity.

Thomson goes on to tell how the intrusion grew worse and worse in spite of all efforts to prevent it.

"In short, so little effect had this, that those who had been spared were spirited up to stay, and others went and settled by them, so that in a few years the settlements in the Indian country were more numerous and farther extended than ever. (Page 73.)"

In another of his outbursts, the Judge says:—

"From Mr. Fisher's standpoint, it is a fact worthy of being recorded on the page of history that no Scotch-Irish of the settlement joined Bouquet's ranks ; but from his standpoint it is a fact too insignificant for mention that in the previous campaign this same settlement sent twenty-five hundred of its chosen men, under the lead of John Armstrong, to march in the van of Forbes' army to the Ohio."

The whole number of Pennsylvania troops that went with Forbes to the Ohio was twenty-seven hundred, and if I had known that all of them but two hundred came from the Kittochtiny Valley alone, I should certainly have been delighted to enrich my book with such a wonderful statement. But I did not know it and I do not know it yet. I cannot find any one competent to judge of such things who ever heard of it. I have asked some of the gentlemen at the Historical

Society, men who have spent their lives in studying the colonial history of Pennsylvania, and they laughed at it.

The Judge scarcely does justice to the other Scotch-Irish in Pennsylvania. Is it possible that if the eight thousand people of the Kittochtiny Valley sent twenty-five hundred, the other thousands of Scotch-Irish outside of the valley and scattered all over the State sent only two hundred?

And then what becomes of the Germans? They were far more numerous in Pennsylvania than the Scotch-Irish. And what becomes of the English Presbyterians, the Episcopalians, and the plain Scotch, all of whom were very earnest against the French and Indians? If the Judge will take the trouble to look at the few broken and incomplete lists of companies that were enlisted in the year 1758 and are collected in Pennsylvania Archives, vol. II., second series, pages 549, &c., he will see, as he reads along, many German names, and in the few instances where the residences are given he will find that the troops came from all parts of the State.

In one of the companies the residences are given after quite a number of the names, and I have counted them—one from Virginia, one from New Jersey, two from Delaware, two from Lancaster, four from Philadelphia, four from Maryland, eighteen from Chester, and one from Cumberland.

As I have said, these records are not perfect. They do not give all the troops, and those that are given are incomplete. But they were all that could be found. If that careful study of which he tells us has brought into the Judge's possession the missing records showing exactly where all the soldiers of that year came from, the Historical Society or the department at Harrisburg will be very glad to receive them, or to be allowed to copy them. They will be the most important information that has been received for many a year, and the genealogists will be delighted.

The Judge's twenty-five hundred is too large a proportion, even for the population of his valley, which he says was eight thousand. Supposing that he is right for once in something and that eight thousand was the correct population of the valley, twenty-five hundred would be more than a fourth of the people and almost a third. A fifth is as large a proportion of military men as any community is supposed to furnish. But a fifth is merely the theoretical estimate of political economists, gives the voting element more accurately than the military element, and is seldom obtained in practice. Moreover the Judge says that the twenty-five hundred were "chosen men," and therefore they could not have included the boys and old men who would of necessity have "marched in the van" with Forbes if more than a fourth of the population left their homes.

The whole population of Pennsylvania, at that time, was two hundred thousand. So the Judge would have us believe that the eight thousand people of his happy valley furnished twenty-five hundred of the twenty-seven hundred men, and the remaining one hundred and ninety-two thousand of the people of the province furnished only two hundred.

The scenes of many of Trollope's novels are laid in an imaginary county, of which he had drawn a map for himself with the residences of all his characters on it; and he boasts in his autobiography that he had added a new county to England. The Judge has added a new valley to Pennsylvania.

By the way, what does he mean by saying that his twenty-five hundred "marched in the van of Forbes' army"? Besides the Pennsylvania troops, that army of about seven thousand men was composed of British regulars, Virginia troops, Maryland troops, and North Carolina troops. If the Judge has any information about the order of march in that scramble through the woods and mountains which Parkman so vividly describes, his Scotch-Irish generosity should furnish us with it, for it would be extremely interesting.

Does he mean that his twenty-five hundred were alone given the honor of the van because their valley had broken all the records of history, and that the remaining two hundred Pennsylvanians were in the rear? Or did all the Pennsylvanians always march in the van? Proud honor for our State it would be; and if it is true, let us have the authority. Parkman, relying on a description by one of the officers, in the *Gentleman's Magazine* (vol. XXIX., page 171), says that when the army was approaching Fort Pitt the provincials were on one of the wings, apparently the left wing.

I have already said that the Judge claims Provost Smith as a Scotch-Irishman. But he was not. He was a Scotchman, born in Scotland, and educated at the University of Aberdeen, and never lived in Ireland. It might also possibly be inferred from what he says that James Wilson was Scotch-Irish. But he also, like Smith, was a Scotchman who had never lived in Ireland.

He says, however, that Wilson's "casting vote placed Pennsylvania on the side of the Revolution." I suppose he must refer to the vote taken in the Continental Congress in adopting the Declaration of Independence. But Wilson's biographers do not claim this honor for him.

According to the account of Wilson, given in the "Biography of the Signers" (vol. VI., page 133), the first vote of the Pennsylvania delegation was: Franklin, Wilson, and Morton, yes; Humphreys, Willing, Robert Morris, and Dickinson, no; so Pennsylvania, on that vote, stood opposed to the adoption of a Declaration of Independence. On the final vote, however, Dickinson and Robert Morris were absent and not voting, so it stood Franklin, Wilson, and Morton, yes; Humphreys and Willing, no. Wilson's vote was no more a casting vote than Franklin's or Morton's, and the vote was carried in the affirmative by the absence of Morris and Dickinson, who had previously voted no.

I must also protest against Dr. Robert Ellis Thompson, who said in his speech that I describe the Scotch-Irish as scattering in the mountains and going nowhere else in the State. I will quote what I said:—

"They did not, however, all seek the frontier, as has been supposed; many of them, especially in Pennsylvania, remained in the East. In modern times many of them have settled in the southwestern section of Philadelphia. * * * They scattered themselves to some extent all over the State, and members of the race can now be found in almost every part of it. A large number of them went up on the Lehigh. Some of the first arrivals went into Bucks County and Lancaster County. They also occupied Octorara Creek, Pequea, Donegal, and Paxton. ('Making of Pennsylvania,' page 163.)"

Several of the speakers at the banquet said that the New England people had been allowed to write the history of the country long enough, and had written it too much in their own way, and that it was now time for the Scotch-Irish to write it in their way. Well, if the report of Judge Stewart's speech is a sample of the way the Scotch-Irish will write history, our fate is a sad one. I think an apology is due from the Society to the whole country for allowing such ridiculous statements to masquerade under the name of history in the printed report of their proceedings.

The reason that the New Englanders have been able to write the history of the country, and that the others have not, is because that, while taking care of their own point of view, they have written on the whole with reasonable accuracy, while the others have usually produced miserable trash for which no one has any respect and which few care to read.

I have no dislike for or antipathy to the Scotch-Irish. On the contrary, I admire them when they behave themselves; especially the old type who were usually right with their facts, and I believe most people admire them. In my two books on Pennsylvania, I have given them full credit for all their merits, and as I was writing history, and not making after-dinner speeches, I have set down likewise their defects and mistakes; and I have treated the Germans, the Welsh, the Episcopalians, the Quakers, and the Connecticut element in the same way. If I have done injustice to any of these elements of our population, either in too much praise or too much blame, I should be glad to know it.

The complaint the Scotch-Irish are continually making, that their merits are not appreciated by the world, I cannot understand. I have never seen any signs of it. Their merit was recognized one hundred years ago and is to-day. They played their part well, and we all know what it was. What people object to is, their claim that they did everything. They did not make the Revolution and the Constitution. Washington, John Adams, Samuel Adams, Jefferson, Henry, Madison, Hamilton, the Lees, the Rutledges, Generals Greene, Gates, Lafayette, Knox, Putnam, Schuyler, Mifflin, and Muhlenberg, were not Scotch-Irishmen, although Armstrong, Stark, Reed, and some others, of good service but minor fame, were Scotch-Irish, and Wayne was descended from an English Episcopalian family who had lived among the Scotch-Irish in

Ireland. The Scotch-Irish had no Tories among them. They were always willing to enlist in the Continental Army, and no one has ever denied it.

People also object to their claiming as their own, men who are not Scotch-Irish at all, and to their claiming distinguished men, who have only a small portion of Scotch-Irish blood in them. On the other hand, I have never heard any one deny the service of the rank and file of the race as frontiersmen in Colonial times, from Pennsylvania to Georgia, afterwards in Ohio, Kentucky, and Tennessee, and in still later times in the religious, industrial, agricultural, and political interests of those same regions.

SYDNEY G. FISHER.

APPENDIX D.

REPORT OF CHARLES L. MCKEEHAN, TREASURER PENNSYLVANIA SCOTCH-IRISH SOCIETY, MADE FEBRUARY 10TH, 1898.

1898. DR.

Feb. 1—Balance from preceding year		$539 19
Dues from members and subscriptions to eighth annual banquet		784 00
Interest on deposits		15 33
		$1338 52

CR.

Hotel Bellevue, eighth annual banquet	$411 45	
Allen, Lane & Scott, printing eighth annual report	175 00	
Stenographer for eighth banquet	30 00	
Louis Dreka, menus	50 00	
William H. Hoskins, invitations and letter heads	18 35	
Allen, Lane & Scott, stationery, bill heads, notices, postage, and clerk hire	54 04	
Postage, expressage	18 50	
Wanamaker & Brown, Pioneer uniform	10 00	
	$767 34	
Balance	571 18	
		$1338 52

CHARLES L. McKEEHAN,
Treasurer.

The above report of the Treasurer has been audited and found correct, showing a balance of $571.18 to the credit of the Society in bank February 1st, 1898.

EDWIN S. STUART,
JNO. A. McDOWELL,
Auditors.

CONSTITUTION AND BY-LAWS.

I. Name.

The name of the Association shall be the "Pennsylvania Scotch-Irish Society," and it shall constitute the Pennsylvania branch of the Scotch-Irish Society of America.

II. Objects.

The purposes of this Society are the preservation of Scotch-Irish history; the keeping alive the *esprit de corps* of the race; and the promotion of social intercourse and fraternal feeling among its members, now and hereafter.

III. Membership.

1. Any male person of good character, at least twenty-one years of age, residing in the State of Pennsylvania, of Scotch-Irish descent through one or both parents, shall be eligible to membership, and shall become a member by the majority vote of the Society or of its Council, subscribing these articles, and paying an annual fee of two dollars: *Provided*, That all persons whose names were enrolled prior to February 13th, 1890, are members: *And provided further*, That three officers of the National Society, to be named by it, shall be admitted to sit and deliberate with this Society.

2. The Society, by a two-thirds vote of its members present at any regular meeting, may suspend from the privileges of the Society, or remove altogether, any person guilty of gross misconduct.

3. Any member who shall have failed to pay his dues for two consecutive years, without giving reasons satisfactory to the Council, shall, after thirty days' notice of such failure, be dropped from the roll.

IV. ANNUAL MEETING.

1. The annual meeting shall be held at such time and place as shall be determined by the Council. Notice of the same shall be given in the Philadelphia daily papers, and be mailed to each member of the Society.

2. Special meetings may be called by the President or a Vice-President, or, in their absence, by two members of the Council.

V. OFFICERS AND COMMITTEES.

At each annual meeting there shall be elected a President, a First and Second Vice-President, a Treasurer, a Secretary, and twelve Directors, but the same person may be both Secretary and Treasurer.

They shall enter upon office on the 1st of March next succeeding, and shall serve for one year and until their successors are chosen. The officers and Directors together with the ex-Presidents of the Society shall constitute the Council. Of the Council there shall be four Standing Committees.

1. On admission; consisting of four Directors, the Secretary, and the First Vice-President.

2. On Finance; consisting of the officers of the Society.

3. On Entertainments; consisting of the Second Vice-President and four Directors.

4. On History and Archives; consisting of four Directors.

VI. DUTIES OF OFFICERS.

1. The President, or in his absence the First Vice-President, or if he too is absent the Second Vice-President, shall preside at all meetings of the Society or the Council. In the absence at any time of all these, then a temporary Chairman shall be chosen.

2. The Secretary shall keep a record of the proceedings of the Society and of the Council.

3. The Treasurer shall have charge of all moneys and securities of the Society; he shall, under the direction of the Finance Committee, pay all its bills, and at the meeting of

said committee next preceding the annual meeting of the Society shall make a full and detailed report.

VII. DUTIES OF COMMITTEES.

1. The Committee on Admission shall consider and report, to the Council or to the Society, upon all names of persons submitted for membership.

2. The Finance Committee shall audit all claims against the Society, and, through a sub-committee, shall audit annually the accounts of the Treasurer.

3. The Committee on Entertainments shall, under the direction of the Council, provide for the annual banquet.

4. The Committee on History and Archives shall provide for the collection and preservation of the history and records of the achievements of the Scotch-Irish people of America, and especially of Pennsylvania.

VIII. CHANGES.

The Council may enlarge or diminish the duties and powers of the officers and committees at its pleasure, and fill vacancies occurring during the year by death or resignation.

IX. QUORUM.

Fifteen members shall constitute a quorum of the Society; of the Council five members, and of the committees a majority.

X. FEES.

The annual dues shall be two dollars, and shall be payable on February 1st in each year.

XI. BANQUET.

The annual banquet of the Society shall be held on the second Thursday of February, at such time and in such manner, and such other day and place, as shall be determined by the Council. The costs of the same shall be at the charge of those attending it.

XII. Amendments.

1. These articles may be altered or amended at any annual meeting of the Society, the proposed amendment having been approved by the Council, and notice of such proposed amendment sent to each member with the notice of the annual meeting.

2. They may also be amended at any meeting of the Society, provided that the alteration shall have been submitted at a previous meeting.

3. No amendment or alteration shall be made without the approval of two-thirds of the members present at the time of their final consideration, and not less than twenty-five voters for such alteration or amendment.

LIST OF MEMBERS.

ALEXANDER ADAMS	1621 Derry St., Harrisburg, Pa.
W. J. ADAMS	Harrisburg, Pa.
HON. J. SIMPSON AFRICA	Union Trust Co., 719 Chestnut St., Phila.
HON. DANIEL AGNEW (Honorary)	Beaver, Beaver County, Pa.
HON. WILLIAM H. ARMSTRONG,	Continental Hotel, Philadelphia.
THOMAS E. BAIRD	214 South Twenty-fourth St., Phila.
JAMES M. BARNETT	New Bloomfield, Perry County, Pa.
JOHN CROMWELL BELL	1001 Chestnut St., Philadelphia.
R. T. BLACK	Scranton, Pa.
P. P. BOWLES	701 Arch Street, Philadelphia.
SAMUEL BRADBURY	Wayne Ave., Germantown, Phila.
SAMUEL R. BROADBENT	3431 Walnut St., Philadelphia.
FRANCIS SHUNK BROWN	815 Stephen Girard Building, Phila.
JOHN W. BUCHANAN	Beaver, Beaver County, Pa.
CHARLES ELMER BUSHNELL	S. E. cor. 4th and Chestnut Sts., Phila.
W. J. CALDER	5 South Second St., Harrisburg, Pa.
J. ALBERT CALDWELL	902 Chestnut St., Philadelphia.
SETH CALDWELL, JR.	1939 Chestnut St. (Girard Bank, Third below Chestnut), Philadelphia.
HON. J. DONALD CAMERON	U. S. Senate, Washington, D. C.
HON. EDWARD CAMPBELL	Uniontown, Fayette County, Pa.
GEORGE CAMPBELL	Washington Ave. and 21st St., Phila.
GEORGE CAMPBELL	Hotel Hamilton, Philadelphia.
HON. J. D. CAMPBELL	P. & R. Terminal, Philadelphia.
ROBERT CARSON	Huntingdon St. and Trenton Ave., Phila.
HENRY CARVER	Harrison Building, Philadelphia.
A. J. CASSATT	Haverford, Pa.
COL. JOHN CASSELS	1907 F St., Washington, D. C.
REV. WILLIAM CATHCART, D. D. (Honorary)	Hoyt, Montgomery County, Pa.
JOHN H. CHESTNUT	636 Drexel Building, Philadelphia.
JOHN H. W. CHESTNUT, M. D.	1757 Frankford Ave., Philadelphia.
A. H. CHRISTY	Scranton, Pa.
JAMES CLARK	Harrisburg, Pa.
ROWAN CLARK, M. D.	112 Logan St., Tyrone, Pa.
CHARLES H. CLARKE	3943 Market St., Philadelphia.
THOMAS COCHRAN	4200 Walnut St., Philadelphia.

REV. DAVID CONWAY . . . . Mount Joy, Lancaster County, Pa.
REV. J. AGNEW CRAWFORD, D. D.
  (Honorary) . . . . Chambersburg, Pa.
ALEXANDER CROW, JR. . . . . 2112 Spring Garden St., Philadelphia.
ROLAND G. CURTIN, M. D. . . 22 South Eighteenth St., Philadelphia.
HON. JOHN DALZELL . . . . . House of Representatives, Washington, D. C.
E. B. DAWSON . . . . Uniontown, Fayette County, Pa.
JOHN B. DEAVER, M. D. . . . 1634 Walnut St., Philadelphia.
JAMES AYLWARD DEVELIN . . 400 Chestnut St., Phila., Wood Building.
REV. CHARLES A. DICKEY, D. D., 2211 St. James Place, Philadelphia.
J. M. C. DICKEY . . . . . . Oxford, Chester County, Pa.
S. RALSTON DICKEY . . . . . Oxford, Chester County, Pa.
A. W. DICKSON . . . . . . Scranton, Pa.
JAMES P. DICKSON . . . . . Scranton, Pa.
DR. JAMES L. DIVEN . . . . New Bloomfield, Perry County, Pa.
J. P. DONALDSON . . . . . . Manhattan Life Building, Fourth and Walnut Sts., Philadelphia.
ROBERT DORNAN . . . . . . Howard, Oxford, and Mascher Sts., Phila.

DANIEL M. EASTER, M. D. . . . 1516 Christian St., Philadelphia.
HON. T. B. ELDER . . . . . Elders' Ridge, Indiana County, Pa.
REV. ALFRED L. ELWYN . . . 1422 Walnut St., Philadelphia.
REV. EBENEZER ERSKINE, D. D., Newville, Cumberland County, Pa.
HON. NATHANIEL EWING . . . Uniontown, Fayette County, Pa.
HON. THOMAS EWING . . . . Pittsburgh, Pa.
SAMUEL EVANS . . . . Columbia, Pa.

EDGAR DUDLEY FARIES . . . . 308 Walnut St., Philadelphia.
HON. JOSEPH C. FERGUSON . . 1423 North Broad St., Philadelphia.
WILLIAM N. FERGUSON, M. D. . 116 West York St., Philadelphia.
JOHN FIELD . . . . Young, Smyth, Field & Co., 816 Market St., Philadelphia.
WILLIAM M. FIELD . . . . . 1823 Spruce St., Philadelphia.
HON. THOMAS K. FINLETTER . 500 North Fifth St., Philadelphia.
WILLIAM RIGHTER FISHER . . Stephen Girard Building, Philadelphia.
D. FLEMING . . . . 325 North Front St., Philadelphia, Pa.
SAMUEL W. FLEMING . . . . 32 North Third St., Harrisburg, Pa.
HON. MORRISON FOSTER . . . Shields, Allegheny County, Pa.
HUGH R. FULTON . . . . . . Lancaster, Pa.
REV. ROBERT H. FULTON, D. D., 3420 Hamilton St., Philadelphia.
HARVEY GRÆME FURBAY . . . The Lorraine, Broad and Fairmount Ave., Philadelphia.

REV. S. A. GAYLEY, D. D. . . . Wayne, Pa.
REV. W. H. GILL, D. D. . . . 1318 South Broad St., Philadelphia.
SAMUEL F. GIVIN . . . . . . 2116 Chestnut St., Philadelphia.

WILLIAM B. GIVIN	224 Locust St., Columbia, Pa.
HON. JAS. GAY GORDON	1628 North Thirteenth St., Philadelphia.
ALBERT GRAFF	4048 Walnut St., Philadelphia.
DUNCAN M. GRAHAM	Carlisle, Pa.
JOHN GRAHAM	Wilkesbarre, Pa.
JOHN H. GRAHAM	533 Drexel Building, Philadelphia.
REV. LOYAL Y. GRAHAM, D.D.	2325 Green St., Philadelphia.
THEODORE R. GRAHAM	1917 Wallace St., Philadelphia.
WILLIAM H. GRAHAM	Mercantile Trust Co., 413 Wood Street, Pittsburg, Pa.
CAPT. JOHN P. GREEN	Pennsylvania Railroad Office, Broad and Market Sts., Philadelphia.
J. M. GUFFY	43 Sixth Ave., Pittsburgh, Pa.
HON. J. MILTON GUTHRIE	Indiana, Pa.
GEORGE T. GWILLIAM	2317 DeLancey Place, Philadelphia.
DR. SAMUEL MCCLINTOCK HAMILL	1822 Spruce St., Philadelphia.
ROBERT S. HAMMERSLEY	Beach and Laurel Sts., Philadelphia.
WILLIAM HAMMERSLY	Broad Street Station, Philadelphia.
HON. WILLIAM B. HANNA	110 South Thirty-eighth St., Philadelphia.
HON. M. A. HANNA (Honorary)	United States Senate, Washington, D. C.
CAPT. JOHN C. HARVEY	Harrisburg, Pa.
HON. DANIEL H. HASTINGS	Harrisburg, Pa.
GEORGE HAY	25 South Water St., Philadelphia.
JAMES HAY	25 South Water St., Philadelphia.
JOHN HAYS	Carlisle, Pa.
REV. I. N. HAYS, D. D.	117 Sheffield St., Allegheny, Pa.
REV. JOHN HEMPHILL, D. D.	2220 Spruce St., Philadelphia.
HON. R. M. HENDERSON	Carlisle, Cumberland County, Pa.
W. M. HENDERSON	Fifth and Columbia Ave., Philadelphia.
CHARLES W. HENRY	Wissahickon Heights, Philadelphia.
HON. J. BAYARD HENRY	701 Drexel Building, Philadelphia.
JOHN J. HENRY	Wissahickon Heights, Chestnut Hill, Philadelphia.
COL. W. A. HERRON	80 Fourth Ave., Pittsburgh, Pa.
A. G. HETHERINGTON	2049 Chestnut St., Philadelphia.
HENRY HOLMES	Trenton Ave. and Auburn St., Phila.
JAMES W. HOUSTON	27 Seventh Ave., Pittsburgh, Pa.
JNO. J. L. HOUSTON	3707 Locust St., Philadelphia.
SAMUEL F. HOUSTON	307 Walnut St., Philadelphia.
JOSEPH M. HUSTON	Witherspoon Building, Phila.
REV. ROBERT HUNTER, D.D.	2828 Frankford Ave., Philadelphia.
B. K. JAMISON	137 South Fifth St., Philadelphia.
JOHN FLEMING JONES	3719 Hamilton St., Philadelphia.
JOHN W. JORDAN	1300 Locust St., Philadelphia, Historical Society of Pennsylvania.

WILLIAM J. JORDAN	804 North Twentieth St., Philadelphia.
GEORGE JUNKIN	532 Walnut St., Philadelphia.
JOSEPH DE F. JUNKIN	532 Walnut St., Philadelphia.
GEORGE C. KENNEDY	38 North Duke St., Lancaster, Pa.
COL. THOS. B. KENNEDY	Chambersburg, Franklin Co., Pa.
M. C. KENNEDY	Chambersburg, Pa.
HON. JAMES KERR	
J. B. KINLEY	Lynwood, Germantown, Philadelphia.
H. P. LAIRD	Greensburg, Pa.
J. A. LANGFITT	110 Diamond St., Pittsburgh, Pa.
HON. JAMES W. LATIMER	York, York County, Pa.
JOHN S. LATTA	1217 Market St., Philadelphia.
WILLIAM J. LATTA	Broad St. Station, Philadelphia.
DR. SAMUEL W. LATTA	3626 Baring St., Philadelphia.
THOMAS LOVE LATTA	3918 Spruce St., Philadelphia.
REV. WM. LAURIE, D.D.	Bellefonte, Pa.
JOHN A. LINN	Radnor, Pa.
JOHN LLOYD	First National Bank, Altoona, Pa.
HARRY V. LOGAN, M.D.	Scranton, Pa.
HON. JAMES A. LOGAN	Broad St. Station, P. R. R., Philadelphia.
JOHN P. LOGAN	826 Drexel Building, Philadelphia.
REV. SAMUEL C. LOGAN, D.D.	Scranton, Pa.
WM. P. LOGAN	826 Drexel Building, Philadelphia.
JAMES LONG	203 Church St., Philadelphia.
REV. J. S. MACINTOSH, D.D.	1334 Chestnut St., Philadelphia.
THOMAS MACKELLAR	612 Sansom St., Philadelphia.
FRANCIS MAGEE	1220 Market St., Philadelphia.
JAMES F. MAGEE	114 North Seventeenth St., Philadelphia.
W. M. MCALARNEY	"The Telegraph," Harrisburg, Pa.
HON. H. J. MCATEER	Alexandria, Huntingdon County, Pa.
HON. ROBERT MCCACHRAN	Newville, Cumberland County, Pa.
HON. SAMUEL J. M. MCCARRELL	Harrisburg, Pa.
J. P. MCCASKEY	"Penna. School Journal," Lancaster, Pa.
W. J. MCCLARY	Wilmington, Del.
DR. C. MCCLELLAND	316 South Eleventh St., Philadelphia.
ALEXANDER K. MCCLURE	"The Times," Eighth and Chestnut Sts., Philadelphia.
JUSTICE J. BREWSTER MCCOLLUM	Girard House, Philadelphia.
R. S. MCCOMBS, M.D.	648 North Eleventh St., Philadelphia.
DR. WILLIAM MCCOMBS	Hazleton, Pa.
HON. A. D. MCCONNELL	Greensburg, Pa.
REV. S. D. MCCONNELL, D.D.	157 Montague St., Brooklyn.
REV. HENRY C. MCCOOK, D.D.	3700 Chestnut St., Philadelphia.
JOHN D. MCCORD	2004 Spruce St., Philadelphia.

EDWARD B. McCORMICK	Greensburg, Pa.
HON. HENRY C. McCORMICK	Harrisburg, Pa.
W. H. McCREA	Carlisle, Pa.
GEORGE D. McCREARY	3301 Arch St., Philadelphia.
M. SIMPSON McCULLOUGH	1717 Spring Garden St., Philadelphia.
JOHN C. McCURDY	2200 North Front St., Philadelphia.
JOHN M. McCURDY	Franklin Building, 133 South Twelfth St., Philadelphia.
REV. O. B. McCURDY	Duncannon, Pa.
J. A. McDOWELL	1727 Walnut St., Philadelphia.
JOHN M. McDOWELL	Chambersburg, Pa.
WILLIAM H. McFADDEN, M.D.	3505 Hamilton St., Philadelphia.
ANDREW C. McGOWIN	1818 Green Street, Philadelphia.
JOHN McILHENNY	1339 Cherry St., Philadelphia.
JOHN D. McILHENNY	1339 Cherry St., Philadelphia.
DR. J. ATKINSON McKEE	1628 Chestnut St., Philadelphia.
CHARLES L. McKEEHAN	2116 Chestnut St., Philadelphia.
JOSEPH PARKER McKEEHAN	Carlisle, Pa.
DR. GEORGE I. McKELWAY	1612 Locust Street, Philadelphia.
GEORGE McKEOWN	506 Library St., Phila. (care of F. H. Bailey).
REV. H. W. McKNIGHT	Pennsylvania College, Gettysburg, Pa.
J. KING McLANAHAN	Hollidaysburg, Pa.
HON. WILLIAM McLEAN	Gettysburg, Adams County, Pa.
ROBERT McMEEN	Mifflintown, Juniata County, Pa.
HON. JOHN B. McPHERSON	Harrisburg, Pa.
DANIEL N. McQUILLEN, M.D.	1628 Chestnut St., Philadelphia.
WM. F. McSPARRAN	Furniss, Pa.
A. W. MELLON	Pittsburgh, Pa.
CHAS. H. MELLON	1734 Spruce St., Philadelphia.
HON. THOMAS MELLON	Pittsburgh, Pa.
GEORGE GLUYAS MERCER	636 Drexel Building, Philadelphia.
JOHN HOUSTON MERRILL	625 Drexel Building, Philadelphia.
JOHN S. MILLER	Harrisburg, Pa.
REV. J. D. MOFFAT, D.D.	President of Washington and Jefferson College, Washington, Pa.
ROBERT H. MOFFITT, D.D.	200 Pine St., Harrisburg, Pa.
EDWARD E. MONTGOMERY, M.D.	1818 Arch St., Philadelphia.
REV. J. H. MUNRO, D.D.	714 North Broad St., Philadelphia.
S. A. MUTCHMORE	Eighteenth and Montgomery Ave., Phila.
H. S. P. NICHOLS	S. E. cor. Sixth and Walnut Sts., Phila.
A. WILSON NORRIS	No. 5 North Market Sq., Harrisburg, Pa.
H. M. NORTH	Columbia, Lancaster County, Pa.
DR. THOMAS J. ORBISON	3537 Locust St., Philadelphia.
D. A. ORR	Harrisburg, Pa.
JOHN G. ORR	Chambersburg, Pa.
WILLIAM B. ORR	421 Wood St., Pittsburgh, Pa.

C. STUART PATTERSON	600 Girard Building, Philadelphia.
D. RAMSEY PATTERSON	525 Drexel Building, Philadelphia.
T. ELLIOTT PATTERSON	501 Franklin Building, Philadelphia.
T. HOGE PATTERSON	1728 Spruce St., Philadelphia.
THEODORE C. PATTERSON	715 Walnut St., Philadelphia.
THOMAS PATTERSON	Carnegie Hall, Pittsburgh, Pa.
R. H. PATTON	Roxborough, Pa.
REV. W. A. PATTON, D. D.	Wayne, Delaware County, Pa.
WILLIAM A. PATTON	Broad St. Station, P. R. R., Philadelphia.
REV. JAMES D. PAXTON, D. D.	2027 DeLancey Place, Philadelphia.
HUGH PITCAIRN, M. D.	206 West State St., Harrisburg, Pa.
ROBERT PITCAIRN	Supt. P. R. R. Co., Pittsburgh, Pa.
JAMES POLLOCK	2226 East Dauphin St., Philadelphia.
HON. WILLIAM D. PORTER	Duquesne Club, Pittsburgh, Pa.
HON. WM. W. PORTER	2025 Walnut St., Philadelphia.
HON. WILLIAM POTTER	Stenton Avenue, Chestnut Hill, Phila.
SAMUEL REA	Broad St. Station, P. R. R, Philadelphia.
R. S. REED	Thirty-third and Chestnut Sts., Phila.
Dr. JOHN CALVIN RICE	Cheltenham Academy, Ogontz, Pa.
CRAIG D. RITCHIE	637 Walnut Street, Philadelphia.
HON. JOHN B. ROBINSON	Media, Pa.
REV. THOMAS H. ROBINSON, D.D.,	Western Theological Seminary, Ridge Ave., Pittsburgh, Pa.
JAMES SLOCUM ROGERS	Fortieth and Spruce Sts., Philadelphia.
TALBOT MERCER ROGERS	Fortieth and Spruce Sts., Philadelphia.
J. E. RUTHERFORD	Harrisburg, Pa.
W. F. RUTHERFORD	P. O. Box 104, Harrisburg, Pa.
CHARLES SCOTT	1520 Arch St., Philadelphia.
CHARLES SCOTT, JR.	Overbrook Farms, Philadelphia.
JOHN SCOTT, JR.	2218 Locust St., Philadelphia.
JOHN B. SCOTT	1520 Arch St., Philadelphia.
WILLIAM H. SCOTT	1211 Clover St., Philadelphia.
J. A. SEARIGHT	Uniontown, Pa.
T. B. SEARIGHT	Uniontown, Pa.
WALTER KING SHARPE	Chambersburg, Pa.
W. C. SHAW, M. D.	135 Wylie St., Pittsburgh, Pa.
CHAS. T. SHOEN	Hotel Stratford, Philadelphia.
HON. J. W. SIMONTON	Harrisburg, Pa.
REV. DAVID M. SKILLING	Harrisburg, Pa.
CHAS. H. SMILEY	New Bloomfield, Perry Co., Pa.
FRANK W. SMITH	134 South Twentieth St., Philadelphia.
REV. S. E. SNIVELY, M. D.	Sixty-third and Market Sts., Phila.
HON. ROBERT SNODGRASS	13 North Third St., Harrisburg, Pa.
E. J. STACKPOLE	Harrisburg, Pa.

John B. Stauffer . . . . . . Broad Street Station, Philadelphia.
Rev. William S. Steans . . . Washburn St., Scranton, Pa.
Rev. James D. Steele . . . . 29 West Ninety-third St., New York.
Justice James P. Sterrett . . 3800 Walnut St., Philadelphia.
George Stevenson . . . . . . 238 West Logan Square, Philadelphia.
John B. Stevenson, Jr. . . . Abington, Montgomery County, Pa.
George H. Stewart . . . . . Shippensburg, Pa.
Hon. John Stewart . . . . . Chambersburg, Franklin County, Pa.
Rev. George B. Stewart . . 215 North Second St., Harrisburg, Pa.
Samuel C. Stewart . . . . . 1429 Moravian St., Philadelphia.
William M. Stewart . . . . 2008 Walnut St., Philadelphia.
Wm. Shaw Stewart, M.D. . . 1801 Arch Street, Philadelphia.
William C. Stoever . . . . . 727 Walnut Street, Philadelphia.
Hon. James A. Stranahan . . Mercer, Pa.
Hon. Edwin S. Stuart . . . . Philadelphia, Pa.

William Thompson . . . . . 233 South Thirty-ninth St., Philadelphia.
Frank Thomson . . . . Broad St. Station, P. R. R., Philadelphia.
William Thomson, M. D. . . . 1426 Walnut St., Philadelphia.
M. Hampton Todd . . . . . 133 South Twelfth St., Philadelphia.

Samuel Hemphill Wallace . Broad Street Station, Philadelphia.
Thomas L. Wallace . . . . . P. R. R. Freight Station, Harrisburg, Pa.
William S. Wallace . . . . 812 Girard Building, Philadelphia.
William W. Wallace . . . . 1510 Chestnut Street, Philadelphia.
Rev. Frank T. Wheeler . . New Bloomfield, Perry County, Pa.
William Wigton . . . . . . New York City.
James S. Williams . . . . . 711 Drexel Building, Philadelphia.
Justice Henry W. Williams . Continental Hotel, Philadelphia.
Prof. J. Clark Williams . . Pittsburgh, Pa.
Rev. David Wills . . . . . . Disston Memorial Church, Tacony, Pa.
Alexander Wilson, M. D. . . 1863 North Front St., Philadelphia.
M. J. Wilson, M. D. . . . . . 1750 Frankford Ave., Philadelphia.
Cyrus E. Woods . . . . Greensburg, Pa.
D. Walker Woods . . . . . Lewistown, Pa.
Hon. Joseph M. Woods . . . Lewistown, Pa.
Richard W. Woods . . . . . Carlisle, Pa.
John W. Woodside . . . . . 2107 Spring Garden St., Philadelphia.
Rev. Nevin Woodside . . . . 25 Granville St., Pittsburgh, Pa.
William H. Woolverton . . 1323 Broadway, New York.
Hon. Richardson L. Wright . 4308 Frankford Ave., Philadelphia.

Hon. Harman Yerkes . . . . Doylestown, Pa.
Hon. John Russell Young . . 2034 Arch St., Philadelphia.

DECEASED MEMBERS.

Hon. Joseph Allison .... Philadelphia, Pa.
John Baird......................... Philadelphia, Pa.
J. C. Blair .... Huntingdon, Pa.
Rev. Charles Wesley Buoy, D. D........ Philadelphia, Pa.
Hon. Andrew G. Curtin............... Bellefonte, Pa.
William Crossley.................... Philadelphia, Pa.
William Holmes .... Pittsburgh, Pa.
H. H. Houston....................... Philadelphia, Pa.
Hon. R. A. Lamberton .... Harrisburg, Pa.
John Mundell .... Philadelphia, Pa.
C. Watson McKeehan .... Philadelphia, Pa.
James McKeehan .... Newville, Pa.
James E. McLean .... Shippensburg, Pa.
William B. Orr .... Pittsburg, Pa.
James Crowell Pinkerton .... Wayne, Pa.
John P. Rutherford .... Harrisburg, Pa.
Hon. John Scott..................... Philadelphia, Pa.
John B. Scott .... Philadelphia, Pa.
A. Brady Sharpe .... Carlisle, Pa.
John A. Thomson .... Wrightsville, Pa.
Hon. William A. Wallace. .... Clearfield, Pa.
Hon. David Wills .... Gettysburg, Pa.
Col. John A. Wright................. Philadelphia, Pa.

www.ingramcontent.com/pod-product-compliance
Lightning Source LLC
Chambersburg PA
CBHW020058170426
43199CB00009B/324